I0817327

DAVID BOWIE

Forever and Ever

An Illustrated Biography

CLAUDIO FABRETTI

4880 Lower Valley Road • Atglen, PA 19310

I don’t know where
I’m going, but I promise
I won’t be boring.

| DAVID BOWIE

CONTENTS

INTRODUCTION

"I would never have expected, at my age, to have such a hunger for life. I thought, like all great romantic heroes, that I had given everything. But nothing has changed: I still feel charged." A serene David Bowie expressed himself in this way on his fiftieth birthday.

A testament to vitality that could be applied to his entire existence and even to his death. Because, until the last moment, the English artist remained faithful to the Wildean imperative "life as a work of art," even planning his exit from the scene with perfect theatrical timing. The Starman took his leave from the world at the height of his (rediscovered) popularity, while his testamentary work *Blackstar* had just hit the shops,

IF HIS LIFE WAS A WORK OF ART, HIS DEATH WAS ALSO MANAGED IN A SPECTACULAR WAY

complete with a self-epitaph in the single "Lazarus": "Look up here / I'm in heaven / I've got scars that can't be seen."

Bowie had been fighting cancer for eighteen months, and it was while he was struggling with the disease that he recorded the songs—and the magnificent and disturbing videos—of Blackstar.

Previous page: David Bowie in Los Angeles, 2000

The black star, the final destination and tomb of an artist who since the odyssey of Major Tom's spaceship (*Space Oddity*, 1969) had chased a daydream in space.

A death that nevertheless still seems impossible to us. Perhaps because, like a new Dorian Gray, Bowie has always let his portrait age, never his spirit. Or perhaps because his name has long since been made immortal.

A paradox, for someone who started with the Warholian "fifteen minutes of fame," to then immortalize himself as a hero "just for one day" ("Heroes").

After all, Bowie is the epitome of all the contradictions of rock. No one like him has been able to lay bare the clichés of stardom, the morbid but also hypocritical relationship between idols and fans, the false myth of the rocker's sincerity, ever since the libertarian charge of the glam era regenerated rock in a flood of glitter and sequins, feathers and mascara, boots and space suits. All summed up in a single mask, that of Ziggy Stardust, the androgynous alien with ginger hair, first idolized and then devoured by fans, for one of the most powerful metaphors of show business ever.

Bowie as portrayed by Sukita, wearing the famous vinyl striped suit designed by Kansai Yamamoto, during the Aladdin Sane *tour (1973)*

Starting from that first brilliant intuition, Bowie has made everyone confront the joyful falsity of being an artist and, at the same time, its universality, shaping a new aesthetic canon. Receptive and farsighted at the same time, he was one of the first musicians to conceive of rock as a global art form, opening it up to contaminations with theater, music hall, mime, dance, cinema, comics, and visual arts. Moreover, he never limited himself to the music sheet, allowing himself targeted forays onto film sets and TV and theater stages, in addition to his tireless painting activity, which was also crucial for deciphering his compositional style ("I see everything I do in pictorial terms," he once explained).

With Bowie, every boundary between "high" and "low" culture disappeared, because—according to his own happy definition—"Nijinsky meets Woolworth's." It is thanks to his shows that the stage was set up in apocalyptic scenography, with a decadent yet futuristic aesthetic, a legacy of literary and cinematographic philosophies, but also of the street art of mimes and clowns. And in the musical field, his imprint was fundamental in the evolution of several genres, from glam rock to punk, from new wave to white soul.

Despite the constant transformations, that "rock 'n' Bowie" trademark remains perceptible in all his works

His transformation (made famous by the verses of "Changes") led him over the years to a work of permanent palingenesis. But it would be superficial to reduce it to shallow chameleonism. His changing self reflected, if anything, the anxiety to ride and be ahead of the times, to constantly dismantle and rebuild himself, in search of an authentic essence. With a continuity that the "rock 'n' Bowie" trademark made perceptible in all his works, he pushed himself beyond creative limits, breaking the rules even in the recording studio.

A portrait from the documentary Black Tie, White Noise *by David Mallet (1993)*

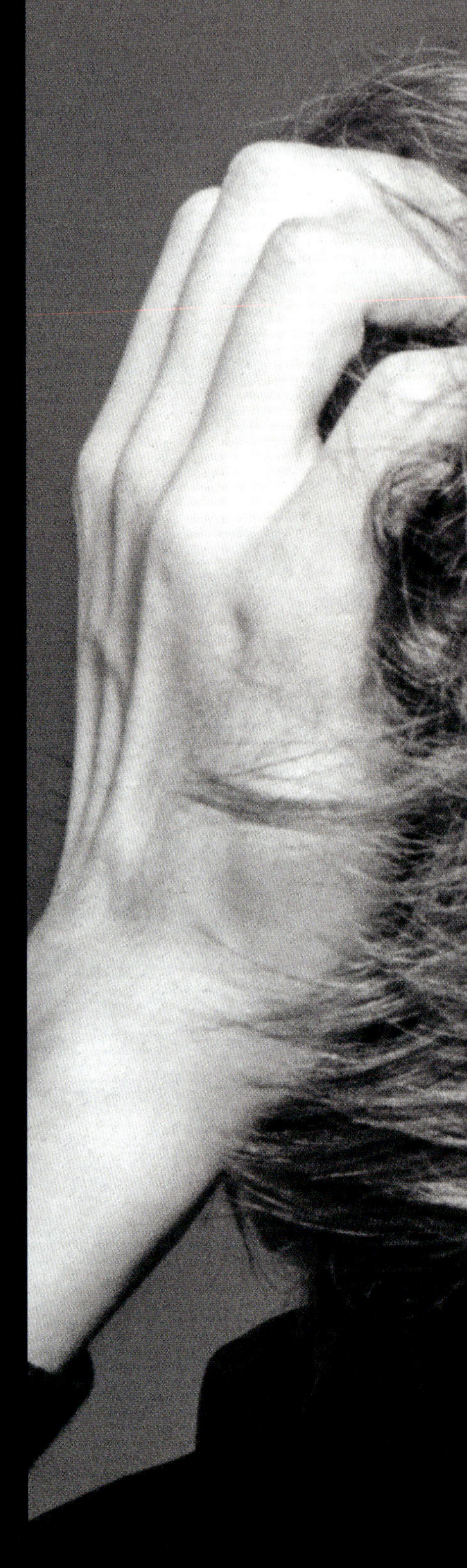

David Bowie photographed by Masayoshi Sukita during the photo sessions for Heroes *(1977)*

An individualistic dandy, an astute media manipulator, Bowie is system and antisystem, the lightness of fashion and the depth of his critical elaboration. He is the mask that becomes a political act (just think of the Orwellian staging of *Diamond Dogs*), the artist in the mirror who tears himself apart in the anguish of his ephemeral time. His characters have been the diaphragm that he has always placed between himself and the world, as well as the most-plausible personifications of his personality. The psych-folk minstrel, the alien Ziggy, the plastic soulman, the icy White Duke, the neoromantic Pierrot, the platinum entertainer, the unscrupulous postindustrial outsider are only the reflections of an elusive identity, which perhaps only in the last period of his life had begun to reveal itself without masks, with an increasingly less transfigured modesty.

But like a film by David Lynch or a play by Bertolt Brecht, Bowie's art does not lend itself to captions. In these pages we will therefore try to put the pieces together, to reconstruct one of the possible paths, without any illusion of authentic explanation. After all, he stated in 1999, "The work of art is complete only when the public adds its own interpretation; it is precisely in that gray intermediate space that its meaning resides." All we can do is try to fill that space. For ever and ever.

Bowie wearing a frock coat designed by Alexander McQueen, backstage at Glastonbury Festival, Worthy Farm, Pilton, in Somerset, UK, June 25, 2000

1

FROM THE STREETS OF BRIXTON TO THE FIRST GLORIES

THE PORTRAIT OF A YOUNG ARTIST: **DAVID JONES** IN SEARCH OF AN IDENTITY

The future Thin White Duke was a son of proletarian London. David Robert Jones was born on January 8, 1947, in the heart of Brixton, a popular and multiethnic neighborhood of the British capital, theater of various social conflicts, which the Clash would immortalize in one of their famous songs ("The Guns Of Brixton").

His portrait as a young man shows a restless middle-class boy, living at number 40 Stansfield Road and making ends meet between studies and dreams, in a gray and degraded London, which still bears the scars of the bombings of the Second World War (1939–1945). His father, Haywood Stenton "John" Jones, recently returned from the front, is employed by a charity organization; his mother, Margaret Mary Burns (called Peggy),

IN SCHOOL, HE IS A BRILLIANT AND RESTLESS STUDENT WHO SINGS IN THE CHOIR AND DANCES AMAZINGLY

works as a cashier at a cinema and has a son from her first marriage, Terry, who suffers from serious mental health problems. David attends Stockwell Infants School until the age of six, acquiring a reputation as a gifted and determined child, as well as an impudent, disrespectful troublemaker.

At that time, a wave of immigration began to change the social fabric of Brixton, shaping the area into the fascinating melting pot that is today. Bowie will spend only the first six years of his life here; despite this, he will maintain a strong bond with his native neighborhood, of which he will remain a symbol, being one of the few Brixton boys to truly achieve world fame.

In 1953, the Jones family moved to Bickley and then to Bromley Common, before settling in Sundridge Park in 1955, where David attended Burnt Ash Junior School. He is a bright and restless pupil, who excels at playing the recorder, sings in the choir, and dances "amazingly for a child," according to his teachers.

He is then enrolled at Bromley Technical High School, where he studies to be a graphic designer. Among his teachers was Owen Frampton, father of Peter, the future famous guitarist and friend of Bowie, who revealed in an interview with Grammy.com: "David and I went to school together. I met him when I was twelve or thirteen. He was a friend of mine, and he was also very close to my father, who was head of the art department of every form of visual art known to man, from typography to fine art! At one point, my father said: 'Well, you guys all play these rock 'n' roll guitars. Why don't you bring them to school and I'll put them in my office so you can play them at lunchtime?' So we did and David became a family friend."

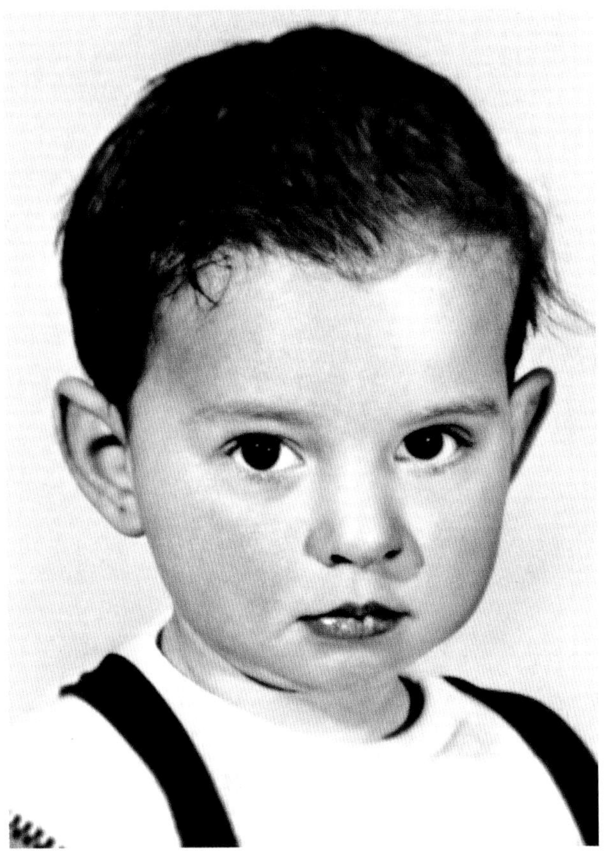

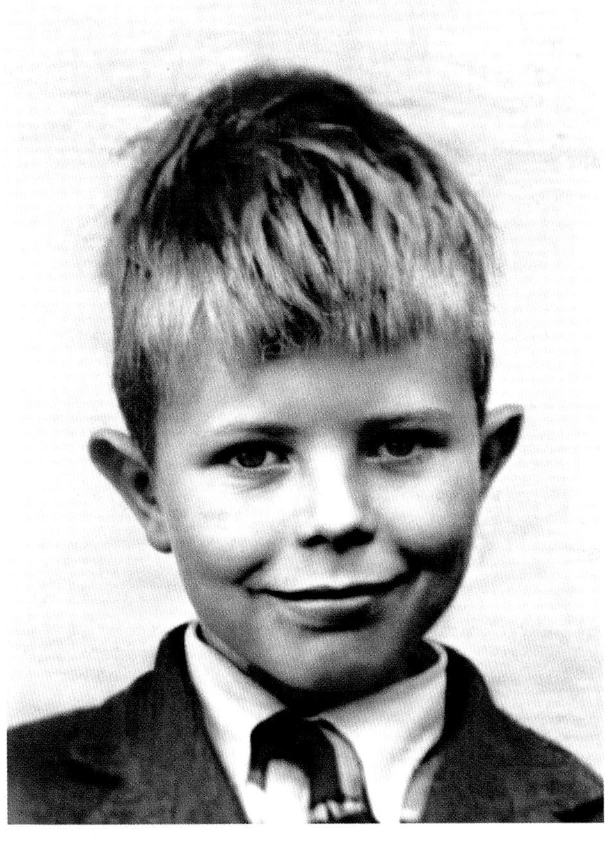

Another schoolmate, the exuberant George Underwood, will instead become the (regretting) protagonist of the most famous boxing match in the history of rock. At the center is Carol, the girl that everyone likes: "We were supposed to meet in a club, but David tricked me and told me that she had changed her mind," Underwood will say. "When I got to the club, his friends said to me: 'Where have you been? Carol waited for you for an hour.' I was 15, and I decided that I would make him pay. The punch I threw wasn't strong, but obviously I had the wrong angle." David suffers a paralysis of the pupil of his left eye, which remains damaged, making him take on that distinctive reddish color that became one of the unique—and magnetic—traits of the future alien of rock.

"I felt terrible for years for having hurt him; it was my cross," Underwood will confess, "but he always thanked me for helping him create his image." A typical Bowie paradox. Their friendship, therefore, will continue without consequences: Underwood will join him in one of his first groups (the King Bees) and will also help him create the artwork for some of his albums. There is an interesting reference to that argument in a 1971 song, "Kooks," in which David will warn his son, Zowie: "And if you ever have to go to school / Remember how they messed up / this old fool / Don't pick fights with the bullies."

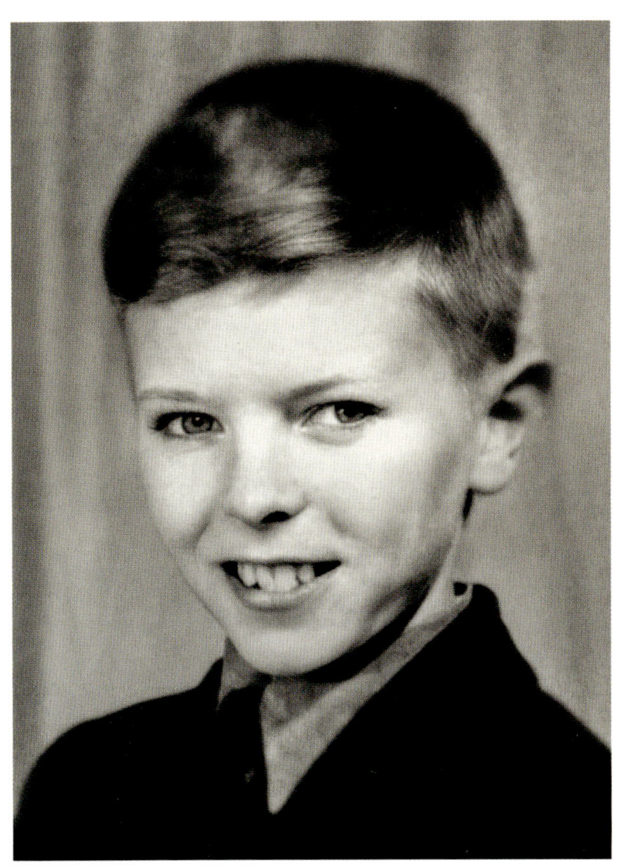

His parents, on the other hand, to quote "Tears for Fears," offer him a "pale shelter": a fragile relationship with his father, who nevertheless encourages him to pursue his musical passion, which was born also thanks to his collection of rock 'n' roll 45s. While with his mother, David develops a more conflictual and not very loving relationship, as we learn from the 2022 documentary *Moonage Daydream*.

Certainly, the turmoil of adolescence sharpens a sense of alienation and diversity that distances him from the common experiences of many of his peers, pushing him to increasingly retreat to his interests, between artistic vocation and spiritual research. Not yet of age, he begins to attend the Buddhist Society of London, remaining fascinated by concepts such as the impermanence and malleability of the mind, principles that he will then, in fact, transform into essential elements of his creative path.

Four images of David Jones as a child, during his school years in London. Bowie attends Stockwell Infants School until the age of six, then Burnt Ash Junior School, becoming a smart and restless pupil.

1962

David Jones, fifteen (third from the left, middle row), *photographed with his classmates at Bromley Technical High School in London*

Having abandoned his studies and tried with little luck to gain experience in one of the many advertising agencies in London, the young Jones allowed himself to be increasingly ensnared by the charm of music. "I was always sleepy; I fell asleep on the drawing boards," he would tell *Les Inrockuptibles*, "because I spent my nights clubbing. I wanted nothing more than clubs. I went both for the experience and to fill my ears. For the loud volume, to listen to Georgie Fame, to discover jazz." He was also dragged along by his older—by ten years—half brother Terry Burns, who suffered from schizophrenia and epileptic seizures that forced him to frequently be admitted to psychiatric wards. During the times spent with David, however, he revealed himself to be an authoritative and charismatic presence: He introduced him to many of the influences that would mark his life, such as modern jazz, Buddhism, beat poetry, and the occult. Jazz was an unstoppable wave for the future Thin White Duke: His enthusiasm for musicians such as Charles Mingus and John Coltrane prompted his mother to buy him a Grafton saxophone in 1961 and to enroll him in lessons with baritone saxophonist Ronnie Ross.

His half brother Terry will be a role model for David, but also a source of anxiety, due to his fragile mental health.

Legend has it that the idyll with rock was born in 1956, when he saw his cousin Kristina dance unrestrained to the tune of Elvis Presley's "Hound Dog." "David and I danced like possessed elves," she would later say. For a kid in the early '60s, there was no shortage of role models: from rock 'n' roll legends like Chuck Berry, Bill Haley, Fats Domino, and, above all, Little Richard ("I heard God," he would exclaim after listening to his "Tutti Frutti"), to the glittering Swingin' London of the beat era.

England was an inexhaustible hotbed of new bands: the Beatles, the Rolling Stones, but also the Who, the Kinks, Pink Floyd, Animals, Yardbirds. It's the invincible army of the "British Invasion" that will also overwhelm the other side of the Atlantic.

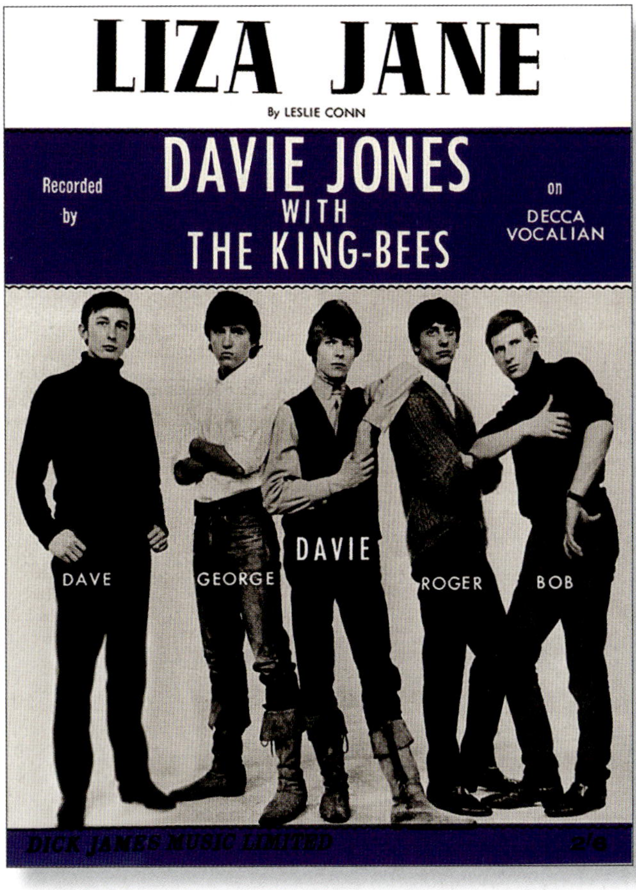

"My son will also become a musician," David's father proudly announces, introducing him to the artists of the Royal Variety Performance.

To make it big, all that was left was to test oneself onstage. And the London nights offered tempting opportunities. David Jones sang and played the sax as the head of a series of underground groups. At fifteen, he forms his first band, the Konrads, but soon moves on to the King Bees, with whom he records his first bluesy 45, "Liza Jane." Then he jumped on a new band, the Manish Boys, another group devoted to the blues with folk and soul nuances, giving birth to a single 45 with two songs recorded in just two hours with the young session man Jimmy Page, future Led Zeppelin guitarist, on lead guitar: a calligraphic version of the blues classic "I Pity the Fool" by Bobby Bland, and a song of his own, "Take My Tip," between jazz and R&B. But it was another flop. He then joined the Lower Third, a mod band heavily influenced by the Who and the Kinks, with whom he released his first single credited to his alias Bowie: "Can't Help Thinking About Me." It was his manager Kenneth Pitt who suggested that he adopt the surname Bowie (from the bowie knife) to avoid confusion with Davy Jones of the Monkees. And after a brief stint in Buzz (with the beat R&B double "Do Anything You Say"-"Good Morning Girl" and the subsequent "I Dig Everything"), it is with his new moniker that he signs his first solo album, *David Bowie*, published by the Deram label in June 1967.

Left: David Jones with one of his first bands, Konrads, in 1963
Above: The cover for "Liza Jane" (1964), 45 LP by David Jones with the King Bees, another of his first bands

BBC TELEVISION CENTRE

Left: David Jones, outside the BBC studios with his band the Manish Boys, before performing "I Pity the Fool" in the Gadzooks! It's All Happening *show. Producer Barry Langford insisted that David cut his hair, but was overruled.*
Above: Onstage with his band the Lower Third

At first, however, the solo adventure struggles to take off. Bowie has matured as a singer, but he still can't decide between the main path of British folk (and Bob Dylan), the psychedelic temptations of the Californian Summer of Love, and the British rhythm 'n' blues revival. His debut on LP unmasks these contradictions, showing a talented but still- immature singer-songwriter, distant from two almost-contemporary colleagues such as Cat Stevens and Al Stewart, who were making their debut in that same period in London. He is all "over the place," as sound engineer Gus Dudgeon defines him: He tries to draw from everywhere without managing to develop a unified and recognizable style.

Above: David Bowie in the cover of his first album, released by Deram in 1967
Right: An image from the same photographic shoot

His clownish acting, close to the style of Anthony Newley (the actor who at that time was taking the West End theaters by storm with the musical *Stop the World – I Want to Get Off!*) permeates ballads such as "Uncle Arthur," "Rubber Band," "and Love You till Tuesday." But they are little more than artisanal divertissement.

The most genuine testimony of this Bowie is, if anything, the *Deram Anthology*, which, in addition to his best song of this period ("The London Boys"), includes the quirky "The Laughing Gnome" (with the sped-up voice like that of a gnome), the vaudeville of "The Gospel According to Tony Day," and a first, embryonic version of "Space Oddity."

Despite the London hangover, Bowie is confused and restless; he feels like a foreign body to his generation; he is light-years away from the trendy hippie ideologies and still seeks refuge in the Buddhist religion: He thus spends three months of monastic isolation with four Tibetan lamas in Scotland, with his partner Hermione Farthingale, to whom he will dedicate a song in his next album, *Space Oddity* ("Letter to Hermione").

But the frail folksinger continues to absorb musical experiences of every genre and style like a sponge of omnivorous thirst. What strikes him in particular is a record released in 1967, branded with a banana on the cover signed by Andy Warhol, the master of pop art. It is titled *The Velvet Underground & Nico* and is the debut album of the revolutionary band of his future friend Lou Reed. "I thought they were the best band in the world," Bowie later confided to *Vanity Fair*, revealing the beginning of an elective affinity with the New York band that would accompany him throughout his career.

The Velvet Underground's dark liturgies dazzle the London artist, who ends up calling them "the best band in the world."

But there is another flash of inspiration—of a cinematic nature, this time—because to Bowie there are no barriers among the arts, and each one of them contributes to influencing his overall vision. It is 1968, and in the darkness of the Casino Cinerama in London, the twenty-one-year-old David stares at the space capsule floating in the void on the big screen. It is the third time he goes to see the film *2001: A Space Odyssey* by Stanley Kubrick, released in April 1968. The sense of alienation of the film is welded to the fascination of science-fiction narrative, at the height of the neopositivist climate that was generating the USA-USSR space competition and that a year later would bring Man to the Moon: a virtuous short circuit for the future Starman. "It was the sense of isolation I was feeling at the time," he told *Classic Rock* magazine in 2012. "It was a real revelation. I composed the song in my head." And what a song! "Space Oddity" is the single that catapulted the young London artist into the orbit of the charts on July 11, 1969. It was the turning point in his career.

Bowie had recorded a first demo in late 1968 for the promotional video of "Love You till Tuesday." That version, which sees him imitating the sounds of a spaceship, turns out to be a commercial flop but offers him the opportunity to sign a recording contract with Mercury. It is the opportunity to record a complete and definitive version of the song. Bowie tries in vain to involve his friend producer Tony Visconti, who will assist him and direct him for much of his career. But Visconti is skeptical and decides to give up, leaving the bizarre experiment to be handled by a young colleague of his, Gus Dudgeon.

Years later, Visconti would regret his intransigence: "I thought the song was a moneymaking commercial about the first moon landing, and it seemed out of line with the folk-rock style of the record. I've kicked myself many, many times since then, because I was completely wrong." Yes, because the majestic "Space Oddity" will remain one of Bowie's greatest hits and an absolute rock classic, with its seven distinct sections, Paul Buckmaster's symphonic-psychedelic arrangements, and a structure similar to the reproduction of the sound of a rocket taking off. Recorded on June 20, 1969, at the Trident studio in London, the song is conceived with surgical precision: the sinister start, punctuated by Bowie's voice lost in space, then the sudden jolt of the stylophone, the timely entrance of Herbie Flowers's bass and Rick Wakeman's (keyboardist from Yes) Mellotron, an epic and poignant chorus, and finally the dissonant instrumental coda. The airy chords, however, betray two unsuspected influences: Simon & Garfunkel and the Bee Gees.

Centered on the saga of the imaginary astronaut Major Tom, "Space Oddity" is the forefather of that science-fiction genre that will become one of the keystones of Bowie's repertoire. The infinite cosmos as a metaphor for an internal space: "Those themes and characters had the metaphysical function of expressing how alienated I was," Bowie explained in 1997 "of communicating that I felt alien to society and that I was looking for some form of connection." These are all concepts that reflect his existential anxiety, the anguish of mortality and oblivion, the permanent conflict between rationality and esotericism, secularism and spirituality: with that memorable injunction of the Control Base ("Check ignition and may God's love be with you") to act as an almost ideal synthesis of these contrasting aspects of his personality. The song was released on July 11, 1969, nine days before the Apollo 11 moon landing, and the BBC used it as the soundtrack for its television programs on the subject. Its success (no. 5 in the UK) would push Bowie to even make versions in other languages, including the unlikely Ragazzo solo, *ragazza sola*, with lyrics by Mogol, for the Italian market.

Lindsay Kemp in Flowers, *onstage at the Polytechnic Theatre in London, 1974. The British choreographer, actor, dancer, mime, and director was one of Bowie's masters.*

The album *Space Oddity* does not add much of significance, except for the aforementioned serenade of "Letter to Hermione" (dedicated to his first partner), destined to remain one of the few explicitly love lyrics of his career, and the epic-folk fairy tale of "Wild Eyed Boy from Freecloud," which will become a live warhorse. The nine-plus minutes of "Cygnet Committee," on the other hand, are above all an example of Bowie's foresight, celebrating in advance the decline of the hippie era and even hinting at punk omens (Could the "guns of love" in the chorus be the future Sex Pistols?).

Bowie also grew as a singer and performer. The meeting with mime-dancer Lindsay Kemp on July 14, 1967, was decisive, the first act of a long collaboration. Bowie attended his courses and was involved in the staging of his show *Pierrot in Turquoise*, onstage in some English offstage theaters until March 30, 1968. "From him," he would say, "I learned body language; I learned to control every gesture, to charge every movement with dramatic intensity; in short, I learned to be onstage."

In the meantime, irreconcilable disagreements will lead to the end of his partnership with manager Ken Pitt: It will be up to the more aggressive Tony Defries to manage a growing talent, even if still a bit naive and awkward, with those effeminate and irreverent looks that divide the teen audience of Britain. "It was a difficult situation," Bowie will say. "In 1969 I had to play in front of very young hooligans who, when they saw me arrive onstage with curls and tracksuit, a bit like Bob Dylan, whistled at me to stop me from playing. They even threw cigarettes at me. This pushed me to leave the big circle; I was completely paranoid." Nothing, however, could slow down the creativity of this rock alien who, in league with Defries, not only did not give up his transformism but even went so far as to accentuate it in a theatricality of shock and transvestism that was increasingly bold and provocative, which would generate the legendary creature Ziggy Stardust.

In the meantime, however, his race to success suffers a setback, due to the death of his father from pneumonia. Exhausted and in a precarious psychological condition, Bowie goes to Beckenham, where he meets the American Angela Barnett, whom he will marry on March 20, 1970: a meeting favored by their common acquaintance of Calvin Mark Lee, director for Europe of the A&R division of Mercury Records in New York. This would be the infamous "three-way relationship" to which Bowie would allude a few years later, defiantly declaring that he had met his future wife when "we were both going out with the same man."

The passionate start of the marriage is sealed by the song "The Prettiest Star," released as a 45 the same month as the wedding in a version featuring his friend-rival Marc Bolan on guitar, which will later be rerecorded and included in *Aladdin Sane* (1973): a declaration of love to his wife, who in that period works hard to help him, keeping in touch with promoters, preparing concerts, and generally taking care of public relations. The marriage will last ten years, giving Bowie, in 1971, his son, Zowie, who would later take the name Duncan Jones, establishing himself as a film director.

Left: A portrait of David Bowie, made in 1969, used for the cover of The Prettiest Star *(above), a loving tribute to his wife, Angela Barnett. It was released as a 45 LP in 1970, with friend-foe Marc Bolan on the guitar. It will eventually be rerecorded and included in* Aladdin Sane *(1973).*

In her books *Free Spirit* (1981) and *Backstage Passes* (1993), Angela Bowie would proudly claim to have played an important role in various aspects of her husband's career, contributing to the androgynous image typical of glam rock. But the relationship between the two soon deteriorated. In a 1993 *Rolling Stone* interview, Bowie said: "We got married because she wanted a work permit in England, which is not a good basis for a marriage. . . . It didn't last very long. By 1974, we were barely seeing each other anymore."

Above: David Bowie boasting a "freak" look with wife, Angie, on their wedding, March 20, 1970

Right: The couple with little Zowie, born May 30, 1971, who would later take the name Duncan Jones, establishing himself as a film director

On the musical side, however, the meeting with guitarist Mick Ronson preludes another fundamental turning point in Bowie's journey. The baptism of fire is on the stage of the Roundhouse in London on the evening of February 22, 1970, with a rock quartet: Bowie, Ronson, and producer Visconti as bassist, plus John Cambridge on drums. They dress up as unlikely superheroes: Rainbowman (Bowie), Gangsterman (Ronson), Hypeman (Visconti), and Cowboyman (Cambridge). They call themselves The Hype, and they pound on their instruments like madmen. Ronson's guitar is their totem, but the one who captures attention is the effeminate singer with curly hair, dressed in multicolored silk robes. It is in such disguise that David Bowie, having buried the shy folk minstrel of his early days, definitively embarks on the path of a sensual and ambiguous rock star, of which the alien Ziggy Stardust will remain the definitive effigy. "Mick was the perfect foil for the character of Ziggy," Bowie will say in an interview in 1994. "He was the classic rough Nordic, with a provocatively masculine personality. He and I were the classic yin and yang. I thought we were as good as Mick Jagger and Keith Richards: We were the personification of that kind of rock 'n' roll dualism."

Mick Ronson becomes the perfect foil for Ziggy Stardust: "Together we were the personification of a Jagger–Richards-style rock duo."

David Bowie with producer Tony Visconti at the Trident Studios in St. Martin's Lane, London, May 1970

Bowie and Ronson locked themselves in the studio with drummer Mick "Woody" Woodmansey and keyboardist Ralph Mace, under the watchful eye of Tony Visconti, now permanent producer/director. The result by the end of the year was *The Man Who Sold the World* (1970), the third album, which effectively marks the beginning of the golden age of Bowie. The new alchemy is a hard and saturated sound, a sort of hard soul-rock, dominated by the rumblings of the bass, the slashes of the guitar, a farsighted Moog (edited by Mace), and Bowie's strangled singing.

Bowie appears for the first time dressed in women's clothes on the cover (censored in the United States) and writes grotesque lyrics, balanced between a horrific futurism ("All the Madmen," "Saviour Machine") and the Nietzschean myth of the Superman ("The Supermen"), whose apex is the paranoid title track, a bizarre meeting between dream and science fiction led askew by the percussion and suspended in oriental atmospheres by the organ and the memorable guitar riff: It will come back more than twenty years later, reinvigorated in Nirvana's new grunge version.

Above: David Bowie wearing female clothes and long blond hair, sprawled on a sofa, in a photo by Keith McMillan, chosen for the cover of the album The Man Who Sold the World *(1970). The long cream-and-blue satin frock came from the London boutique Mr. Fish. Right: The album in its rare, cartoon-style alternative cover*

The debt to the tightrope-walking hard rock of Cream and Led Zeppelin is paid in the riffs of "She Shook Me Cold" and "Black Country Rock," while the journey into the subconscious full of sexual perversions of "The Width of a Circle" will provide Ronson with the inspiration to stage live an electric bacchanal worthy of the Velvet Underground masters.

Perhaps, however, the biggest surprise of the album is "After All," a dark and melancholic waltz, which has the subtle step of the best ceremonials of Iggy Pop's Stooges, another future—and fundamental—acquaintance of Bowie.

The London artist develops an aesthetic that has ambiguity and transformation as its sharpest weapons. And he starts a game of constant provocation with the English press, to which he feeds declarations like "I am homosexual, bivalent, trivalent. I want to try everything." Meanwhile, in order to fulfill the last contractual obligations with his old record company, under the pseudonym of Arnold Corns (a tribute to the first leader of Pink Floyd [Syd Barrett], Arnold Layne), releases a couple of singles. For the occasion, with a twist in full Warholian style, he hands the role of front man to his eccentric stylist Freddie Burretti and publishes a handful of songs (including an embryonic version of "Moonage Daydream" and the allusive title "Man in the Middle"), already dripping with transgression and desire to amaze. Even if the resonance is minimal, it is the prelude to the events that will change his career.

1970

THE FIRST EXPERIMENTS ARE RAW, BUT THEY ALREADY SHOW TRANSGRESSION AND A DESIRE TO SHOCK

Musically, the album marks the first approach to glam rock that exploded in England in the wake of Marc Bolan's T. Rex, under the banner of an ambiguous and irreverent attitude. "Rock 'n' roll with lipstick," John Lennon would rename it. Bowie, who had already anticipated the trend in his previous album, at least in terms of attitude and look, sensed that this could be his stairway to heaven.

But it's not just glam that shines in the grooves of *Hunky Dory*. Carefree pop, sick atmospheres in the style of Velvet Underground, and folk of Dylanian ancestry embellish a record that celebrates the American sociocultural myth through a gallery of characters: from Frank Zappa to Bob Dylan, from Lou Reed to Walt Disney and Andy Warhol. For the occasion, a first-rate cast is brought together. Ronson brings with him the bassist Trevor Bolder and the drummer Mick "Woody" Woodmansey: the future Spiders from Mars. At the wheel, Visconti is replaced by the expert Ken Scott, fresh from the glories of *All Things Must Pass* by George Harrison. Bowie plays guitar, sax, and piano, "as much as his ability allows," as he jokes in the cover notes. For the more elaborate sections, there is a special guest: Rick Wakeman, the tightrope walker-keyboardist of Yes. But the lion's share is taken by Ronson's orchestral arrangements, who, in addition to scratching with the six strings, also reveals himself to be a pianist and a refined musician.

The first masterpiece of the golden decade is *Hunky Dory* (1971), for which manager Tony Defries secures a contract with RCA by flying to New York. The head of the A&R section, Dennis Katz, is enchanted: "It was theatrical, musical . . . the songs were excellent; there was real poetry; it seemed to have everything," he will say. On the cover, a close-up of a melancholic Bowie, who is tidying his flowing blond hair in a fatal pose, like a mix of Lauren Bacall, Greta Garbo, and Marlene Dietrich. The image will be made pictorial with the airbrush and recolored by the infamous Underwood, suggesting the idea of a hand-painted poster from the silent-film era and the famous *Marilyn Diptych* by Andy Warhol. An iconic cover: Even Brian Eno will be struck by it, and, in fact, he will clone it three years later for his LP *Taking Tiger Mountain (by Strategy)*.

This is the album with one of Bowie's manifesto songs, the opening "Changes," which, behind the cocktail-lounge arrangements and the stammered chorus in the style of the Who of *My Generation* ("ch-ch-ch-ch-changes"), hides a bittersweet reflection on the critical changes in life: "Turn and face the strange / Changes / Just gonna have to be a different man / Time may change me / But I can't trace time." The continuous metamorphosis becomes a lifestyle, the incessant anxiety to ride and anticipate the seasons engages in an (impossible) challenge against time, a genuine testimony of the vital, curious, and omnivorous fervor that will distinguish the entire career of the mutant genius from London.

But what will win the hearts of the English public will be one of Bowie's ballads par excellence, promoted by an evocative video clip. If it's the ginger-haired alien Ziggy Stardust to make the myth take off, it's David Robert Jones (still heavily made up like in "Life on Mars?") who will need only a melody on a white background and a disconcerting blue suit (by the ineffable stylist Freddie Burretti) to break through the screen: a surreal film, shot by photographer Mick Rock in 1973, almost disturbing in its staticity, to the point of appearing like a floating pop-art painting. It will also be one of Bowie's first one-man shows, perfectly at ease in that grotesque makeup and in that shocking F sharp, which would have challenged many more celebrated vocalists.

Introduced by the enchanted chords of Wakeman's piano, "Life on Mars?" tells the story of an infamous "girl with mousy hair" grappling with "a God-awful small affair" made of family misunderstandings and celluloid dreams, where even the films soon become "a saddening bore" because she's lived at least ten times. "It's the reaction of a girl sensitive to the world of the media," explained Bowie in 1971, adding, twenty-five years later, "I think she feels betrayed, but, despite living a depressing reality, she is convinced that in some unspecified place there is a life worth living and that she is bitterly dissatisfied by the fact that she doesn't have access to it." The sense of isolation of the protagonist is contrasted by the sonic apotheosis that explodes in the chorus.

Left: The cover for Hunky Dory, *with a close-up of Bowie smoothing his blond locks in the femme fatale style of Lauren Bacall, Greta Garbo, and Marlene Dietrich*

Above: An image from the video of "Life on Mars?"

The guitar and rhythm instruments emerge, but it is above all the breath of the strings that makes its way, amplifying the drama and the melodic grandeur. A theatrical, operatic staging, but everything happens in a perfectly calibrated way by Ronson's genius arrangement, up to the magniloquent crescendo of timpani in the prefinale, which echoes *Also Sprach Zarathustra* by Richard Strauss.

Bowie also shows to have matured as a singer: an example of romantic and cheeky crooner, almost a parody of Frank Sinatra in Cockney sauce, as confirmed by the autographed writing "inspired by Frankie" in the album's cover notes. And in the first eight bars, the song was built precisely on the chord sequence of "My Way." If the title "Life on Mars?" takes its name from an English television show in vogue in the '60s, the lyrics are instead a surreal cutup of characters and eras, images and places, metaphors and evocative stimuli, with consumer society as the common denominator and peaks of witty social denunciation. It is the desolate cross section of the "best-selling show" of a commercial TV that will soon turn into an Orwellian nightmare (from the "ferocious jaws" of 1984's *Diamond Dogs* to TVC 15's *Station to Station*). "Life on Mars?" immediately entered the charts at number 3 and over time became one of the London dandy's greatest hits, even winning the title of Bowie's "greatest song of all time" on BBC Radio 2.

There is no shortage of other feats in the *Hunky Dory* track list: the catchy "Oh! You Pretty Things," all played on the piano and full of new, obscure Nietzschean references; the affectionate dedication to little Zowie on the notes of a vaudeville piano in "Kooks"; the warm and impertinent homages to overseas masters Andy Warhol and "Song for Bob Dylan"; the acoustic sweetness of the poignant "Quicksand,"

DRIVEN BY *"LIFE ON MARS?," HUNKY DORY* CELEBRATES THE AMERICAN SOCIOCULTURAL MYTH, WITH TRIBUTES TO BOB DYLAN AND ANDY WARHOL

which, with its references to Aleister Crowley, reveals one of the darkest sides of the future Thin White Duke. Closing the circle is the cheeky "Queen Bitch," inspired by his stay in the Bowery in New York and—according to many—by the bond with his "American friends" Lou Reed and Iggy Pop, and the dark farewell of "The Bewlay Brothers," psychedelic folk with a circular and claustrophobic structure, reminiscent of

Syd Barrett and the acoustic nightmares of *The Man Who Sold the World*, with lyrics focused on the particular relationship between Bowie and his half brother Terry, including a disturbing prophecy about Burns's suicide, which occurred in 1985: "My brother is lying on the rocks. He could be dead, he could not be, he could be you."

And it could be Bowie himself, who superimposes his own schizophrenia on his brother's, initially exorcised in art but always feared as a family destiny, given the precedents especially on the maternal side: "I never had a clear vision of what Terry's position was in my life, whether he was a real person or whether I was referring to another part of me," Bowie will confide. "I think that's what the song was about." An elusive and enigmatic text, in any case, which ideally closes an album full of disquiet, constantly undermined by the Wildean anguish of impermanence, by the awareness that youthful passion could end up consumed by the inevitable changes and decadence of the years until "no longer having the strength" ("Quicksand") and becoming a "king of oblivion" ("The Bewlay Brothers"). NME would call *Hunky Dory* "Bowie's best album to date," crowning him as "Mick Jagger's heir." And his influence on English pop would be felt for decades, with a host of followers (Marc Almond, Kate Bush, Eurythmics, Blur, and Suede, among many others), while Boy George (Culture Club) would call it "the record that changed my life." It's also the album that's most openly gay-oriented, with explicit lyrics (from "Queen Bitch" to "Oh! You Pretty Things") and an aesthetic borrowed from London's gay subculture, embraced by Bowie during that period. Whether or not it was part of a broader concept of theatricality, this type of sensibility would become an important part of Bowie's universe, where the veil between artifice and reality would become increasingly thin.

But artistic expression and fiction go hand in hand with an introspection that becomes more acute, through a series of recurring themes and obsessions. "It's an album that helped me bring out many aspects of my way of feeling, a lot of schizophrenia," Bowie will admit, who, a year later, to Michael Watts of *Melody Maker*, will reveal that his songs "can be compared to talking to a psychiatrist. Performing is my therapist's chair."

When live, the mutant dandy from Brixton now knows how to dazzle the audience with his magnetic shows and his provocative looks, with gold lamé miniskirts, orange hair, and glitter boots. And thanks to the imaginative power of his songs, he has finally started to win over the critics. But that's not enough for him, because he has only one obsession in his head: "Becoming famous." And he will succeed, with an almost-ferocious determination, closer to the lucid vision of a scientist than to the naive utopianism of post-'68 rockers. While rock celebrates itself in large gatherings, the Warholian Bowie looks at himself in his dressing room in search of the right mask that will enchant the audience. The answer will come from the impossible combination of an interstellar being and an actor from the Japanese Kabuki theater. The first great character of his gallery

2

THE MYTH OF ZIGGY STARDUST AND THE GLAM ERA

THE RISE AND FALL OF THE ALIEN

WHO FREED ROCK

FROM CONVENTION

When the alien Ziggy Stardust falls to Earth, the effect is disconcerting to the point of generating the suspicion that perhaps, this time, things have gone too far. Who would have bet a penny on this extraterrestrial being in tights, with ginger hair and low-end drag queen makeup? A one-of-a-kind creature, impossibly kitsch, who seems to have come out of a trashy science-fiction comic. And yet, it is in his shoes that David Bowie will achieve for the first time that worldwide fame that he had long pursued and never abandoned.

A GINGER-HAIRED ALIEN: THIS IS THE CHARACTER THAT ALLOWS BOWIE TO BREAK DOWN ALL THE CLICHÉS OF ROCK

Even his friend Mick Ronson is doubtful: Legend has it that when Bowie, conceiving Ziggy's space shows, proposed a golden costume, Ronson remained speechless, slipped out the door, and headed for the nearest train station—only to then change his mind the following day. A wise choice, since that very yin-and-yang duo will act as the driving force for one of the masterpieces of the Bowie era.

It is precisely from this brazen transgressive instinct that the glam genre is born. It is the time of the dudes, neohippies who transform the eco-pacifist gatherings of their hippie cousins into an unbridled festival of kitsch. Let it be peace and love, but without any political or ideological constraints. Thus disengagement, transvestism, and sexual ambiguity triumph, in a flood of glitter and sequins, feather boas and mascara, boots and space suits.

David Bowie posing for the camera in June 1972 in London, wearing a jumpsuit and glittering, glam-rock-style platforms designed by his friend Freddie Burretti

It is fertile terrain for dandy Bowie, who feels like he can have a radical impact on this new scene, perhaps moving away from it as soon as it becomes obsolete. "It is probable that it wasn't Bowie who invented glam, but without a doubt it was he who mastered it. Only, unlike Bolan, he then abandoned it," one of his most famous biographers, Nicholas Pegg, will declare.

Initially conceived for a stage musical, Bowie's most famous alien creature takes shape from a melting pot of musical influences. His friend/rival Marc Bolan himself provides a crucial foothold, with his urban science-fiction arsenal and his electrified rock 'n' roll, combined with that way of whispering into the microphone, the makeup, and the poses of a decadent dandy. From the name, then, one can sense the influence of the "Iguana" Iggy Pop, incarnation of the outrageous and animalistic front man, "the wild side of existentialist America" (even if the inspiration also came from a London tailor's shop named called Ziggy's). Then, the lesson of the founding fathers of rock: Little Richard, Gene Vincent, Mick Jagger, and Lou Reed. The latter, in particular, had already left a deep mark: "He gave us the backdrop to set our most-theatrical visions," Bowie explained. "He gave us the streets and the landscape, and we populated them."

Ziggy was born from noble fathers of rock, from unlikely protective gods like Vince Taylor and Legendary Stardust Cowboy, and from the kabuki theater

But other improbable protective spirits were the ones to add the indispensable touch of madness. For example, Vince Taylor, a '60s rocker: "He was firmly convinced that there was a very strong connection between him, aliens, and Jesus Christ," Bowie would later say. "One night he showed up onstage dressed in white, saying that his whole liaison with rock had been a lie, that he was actually Jesus. It was the end of Vince, his career, and everything else." The direct inspiration for "Stardust" came instead from another bizarre character: the American bluesman Legendary Stardust Cowboy, a.k.a. Norman Cal Odam, whose only success had been a 1968 song titled "Paralyzed" and whose fame was based on a disastrous appearance on the television program *Rowan & Martin's Laugh-In*. "Everyone laughed at him and he went away crying," Bowie recalled in 1996. Ziggy is therefore a hybrid of top-end art and delicious tackiness, "when Nijinsky met Woolworth's," as Bowie effectively defined him, entrusting him with the role of the messiah of a rock revolution that would last just one season: the time between his rise and his fall. And in this parable, there is the whole representation of Bowie's art: the staging of the Warholian "fifteen minutes of fame," the morbid hedonism of Dorian Gray, the parody of stardom, the ephemeral myths of

consumer society, and, last but not least, the omens of a dark Orwellian future.

"Extraterrestrial" and therefore free from the sexual taboos that chain humanity, Ziggy Stardust is the quintessence of the glam spirit. Past and future coexist in him: A child of the decadent aura of prewar central European cabaret, he is drawn toward the futuristic impetus of Stanley Kubrick's *A Clockwork Orange* (1971), whose opening notes will open the Ziggy Stardust Tour and whose iconography (the droogs, the costumes, the references to pop art) will profoundly influence the entire saga of the Spiders from Mars.

Last but not least, the influence of kabuki, a type of theatrical performance that arose in Japan in the early seventeenth century, which mixes dramatic performance with traditional dance. "Ever since I began to develop my passion for kabuki," Bowie explains, "it occurred to me that the form of Western entertainment that most closely resembled it was rock."

Ziggy Stardust putting makeup on backstage before a show in London, May 22, 1973. Reflected in the mirror behind him is guitarist Mick Ronson.

1973

Ziggy becomes the mask that embodies all the stereotypes of rock filtered through the bizarre lens of glam. A caricature of the star, destined to be idolized by the public and crushed by the star system. The stage fiction, however, soon prevails over reality, and Bowie will incarnate himself in his alter ego to the point of sacrificing him onstage and making him immortal.

Ziggy Stardust falls to Earth on February 10, 1972, onstage at the Toby Jug, a small concert hall in the London suburb of Tolworth. Accompanying him are the Spiders from Mars; namely, Mick Ronson (guitar), Trevor Bolder (bass), and Mick "Woody" Woodmansey (drums). On this occasion, Bowie presents the songs recorded three months earlier to Trident Studios for his fifth LP, an album that initially does not have a coherent narrative line but will go down in history as the concept album centered on the figure of the alien Ziggy. Or rather, "A human who came into contact with forces from another dimension through his radio, who ends up adopting a messianic role on Earth, mistaking their messages for spiritual revelations."

The famous photo Keep Your 'Lectric Eye *by Masayoshi Sukita in 1973. Bowie is portrayed as a glam icon, wearing an outfit by Japanese designer Kansai Yamamoto and featuring a "futuristic third eye" on his forehead.*

Above and right: David Bowie as Ziggy Stardust during a concert at the Earls Court Exhibition Hall in London, May 12, 1973.

THE

The real love at first sight with the public, however, occurred on a summer night, thanks to the most popular music program on the BBC. It was July 6, 1972, when Bowie's white fingertips emerged from the screens of *Top of the Pops*, intently strumming a blue guitar; then the close-up revealed the red-haired rocker, dressed in a shiny multicolored jumpsuit, surrounded by the Spiders from Mars while he sang the lyrics of his new anthem: "There's a starman waiting in the sky / He'd like to come and meet us / But he thinks he'd blow our minds." "Starman" is the killer single at the right time. The message delivered by the Starman strikes an entire generation of British youth: "The moment he sang 'I had to phone someone, so I picked on you,' Bowie pointed to the camera, and we knew he was singing that line to us and to all the kids who were glued to the show at that moment. It was a real call to arms that put us on the path we would soon follow," the Cure, one of the cornerstone groups of the new wave, would say. Similar words will also return in the testimonies of the new romantic generation included in *Blitzed*, the documentary that narrates another musical season of typically Bowian inspiration.

The performance on *Top of the Pops* is a milestone, comparable in impact to the Beatles' performance on *The Ed Sullivan Show*. And from the Fab Four, in some ways, Starman borrows the prodigious melodic power of that irresistible refrain, supported by Bowie's acoustic guitar and Ronson's violin arrangement. The lyrics, however, renew the attraction for science fiction, spreading a positive message: "The creatures of space are real and human enough, and the prospect of meeting other beings should make us happy," comments Bowie, who has always professed to firmly believe in the existence of extraterrestrial life.

On record, however, the Ziggy Stardust saga opens with an apocalyptic prophecy. The earth is on the brink of collapse; there are five years left before the catastrophe: "We had five years left to cry in" (the dystopian "Five Years"). Lulled by the swing rhapsody of "Soul Love," the listener is then catapulted into a daydream: "Moonage Daydream," the lunar age has arrived, and with it its messiah whose genesis is evoked here: "I'm an alligator, I'm a mama-papa coming for you / I'm the space invader, I'll be a rock 'n' rolling bitch for you." Ziggy is a redeemer, then, but also "a whore," the symbol of the music-business prostitution.

Enhanced by Bowie's shrill falsetto, the mind-blowing distortions of Ronson's Gibson Les Paul, and a lightning-fast sax solo, "Moonage Daydream" is a dazzling electric ride, an apotheosis of pure glam rock that will also give its title to Brett Morgen's definitive film on David Bowie's life.

Bowie's melody style triumphs, not just in Starman, but also in the fluid ambiguity of "Lady Stardust," with Ronson's saturated guitars and poignant piano figures supporting Bowie's crooner-like singing. It's a tribute to Marc Bolan (in the original demo, it was titled "A Song for Marc"), but the "Femme fatales emerged from shadows" lead directly to Lou Reed by Velvet Underground & Nico. The only cover of the album, *It*, is instead signed by Ron Davies's "Ain't Easy," a sort of space country with an almost gospel chorus. To break this dreamy atmosphere of 1930s musicals, a couple of protopunk forays launched at a frenetic speed by the Spiders Martians: "Hang On to Yourself," which by the Sex Pistols' own admission will inspire "God Save the Queen," and "Suffragette City," a hymn to prostitutes complete with a postorgasmic exclamation ("Ohhh, wham bam, thank you, ma'am!"), which will be the soundtrack to Bowie and Ronson's sexual pantomimes onstage during the Ziggy Stardust Tour, the most famous being the one with the infamous "guitar fellatio" immortalized by photographer Mick Rock. It will also be songs like these that will make Gavin Friday of the Virgin Prunes, another cult new wave group, say, "We were all the bastard children of Ziggy Stardust."

Now a star, Ziggy can finally be celebrated by the immortal riff of the title track: Ronson's scratchy guitar underlines the story of the star who "bulged his eyes and tossed his hair like some Japanese cats" but who ended up being devoured by a horde of fan/executioners: "Making love to his ego, Ziggy was sucked into his mind / like a leper messiah / When the boys killed him, I had to break up the band." Bowie disguises himself as a passionate storyteller, but in reality he is behind the scenes, pulling the strings of his creature with aristocratic sarcasm—just as he will do a year later, when, Hamlet's skull in hand, he will dramatize the exploits of his Hollywood Cracked actor in *Aladdin Sane.*

The natural conclusion of the album can only be a "Rock 'n' Roll Suicide," consumed in the most theatrical of ways, begging for a final gesture of affection ("Gimme your hands, because you're wonderful"), which Ziggy will mime in his live shows, going toward the audience. The Spiders from Mars set up another terrifying crescendo, the ideal backdrop for Bowie's hallucinatory and tense singing, in an alienating Brechtian cabaret atmosphere. "Rock 'n' Roll Suicide" is the album's farewell, as well as the song with which, on July 3, 1973, at the end of a London concert, Bowie will announce Ziggy's death.

Left: Bowie performs "The Jean Genie" *on BBC* Top of The Pops, *London, January 3, 1973.*

ZIGGY STARDUST

With a cover photo by Brian Ward showing Bowie with a Greta Garbo-style hairstyle on a rainy Heddon Street in the heart of London, *The Rise and Fall of Ziggy Stardust and the Spiders from Mars* is the musical sublimation of an entire era. The entire glam arsenal shines in the eleven tracks: the emphatic and effeminate voices, the sharp guitars, the pompous string arrangements, the poignant melodies, in an alternation of romantic ballads and very tight electrified rock 'n' roll, precursors of punk. Music to be played full blast, as recommended by the back cover, with always-accurate lyrics, literary references, rich in American expressions not in common use in the England of the time, but often also the result of sardonic transgression and pure nonsense. The entire work is an essay in total art, in which music marries theater, music hall, mime, cinema, comics, and the visual arts, but without ever losing sight of the final goal: fame.

Previous pages: The famous mimed sexual act performed by Bowie on Mick Ronson's guitar, during the tour of Ziggy Stardust
Above: The cover for The Rise and Fall of Ziggy Stardust and the Spiders from Mars, *with a picture by Brian Ward featuring Bowie in Heddon Street, in the heart of London*

If at the beginning its success was confined mainly to the United Kingdom (where it climbed to fifth place in the charts), over the years it expanded on a global scale, exceeding the milestone of seven million copies sold and also obtaining the certification as a gold record on June 12, 1974, by the RIAA in the United States. But, above all, it will remain in history as the record consecrating David Bowie, the one thanks to which the former restless folk singer from

Brixton rose to world stardom. As planned. And yet, in this bonfire of the vanities, the dark side of the planet Mars does not escape: a reflection on alienation and death, on the ephemeral destiny of stardom as a metaphor for the human condition itself. That decaying portrait of Dorian Gray has always obsessed the London artist.

The Ziggy saga went viral all over the world and helped launch glam rock as a universal trend, allowing Bowie to become a producer for his friends Lou Reed (in the splendid LP *Transformer*) and Iggy Pop (on *Raw Power* of his Stooges), as well as author-patron for Mott the Hoople, to whom he gives a guaranteed hit: the rousing generational glam anthem "All The Young Dudes." The "lipstick rock 'n' roll" fever is infecting the UK—bands such as Roxy Music, Queen, Sweet, and Steve Harley & Cockney Rebel, and solo artists such as Rod Stewart and Elton John—but it is also spreading overseas (New York Dolls, Alice Cooper, Suzi Quatro), with transvestism and provocation always acting as a common denominator. Bowie reveals to *Melody Maker* that he has "always been gay," then identifies himself as bisexual live on the BBC, statements that will cause a stir—especially in puritanical America—and that will be retracted over the years in a constant push and pull, which will not, however, call into question his role as the standard-bearer of ambiguity in rock. Even Jim Morrison caused a scandal, even Mick Jagger wore makeup, even the Fugs were obscene, but with Bowie, for the first time, sexuality was freed from all barriers. It became perverse and complex, "from another planet," and therefore undefined and mutagenic: like one of the many costume changes onstage. And, if it seems ultimately irrelevant to dwell on his sexual orientation, it makes more sense to underline his connection with camp culture and with the elevation of the aesthetic aspect over the purely practical, in accordance with the principles of Oscar Wilde and Susan Sontag—an approach that broke the unwritten laws of rock and its supposed sense of spontaneity and sincerity. Bowie fed on artificiality to unmask clichés: "When I'm on stage, I feel like an actor rather than a rock artist," he declared in 1972 to *Rolling Stone*.

A multicolored lightning bolt striking right across the face, a bit of white greasepaint, and a light touch-up of the makeup, and the glam era can continue a year later with *Aladdin Sane*. The title of the new album, which replaces the provisional "Love Aladdin Vein" (deemed too disturbing with its allusion to drugs), is a play on words between "Aladdin sane" and "A lad insane." And the cover remains, to this day, one of the most iconic in the entire history of rock. The crimson- and-blue lightning bolt that splits Bowie's face in two reproduces the internal schism in his personality: The aim of photographer Brian Duffy was precisely to capture the artistic and personal duality inside the soul of the British singer-songwriter at that moment.

Aladdin Sane can be considered the natural sequel to its predecessor, but also a further refinement of that sound. "Ziggy in America," as Bowie will rename it, places the emphasis on the purely rock 'n' roll soul, but also on the lyrics, in which the reality of the States is transfigured in a series of sound panels, now futuristic and hallucinatory, now parodistic or melancholically dreamy.

WITH A MULTICOLORED LIGHTNING BOLT ACROSS HIS FACE, HERE IS *ALADDIN SANE*, A.K.A. ZIGGY'S JOURNEY TO AMERICA

It is the ideal travel diary of the long overseas tour that opened the doors of America to Bowie. Beginning in Cleveland on September 22, 1972, the series of concerts, which should have ended a month later, was extended for a year and a half. A flamboyant Bowiemania thus began to spread in the United States as well, pushed by RCA, which financed the tour with a pharaonic display of resources, including dancers, makeup artists, and bodyguards.

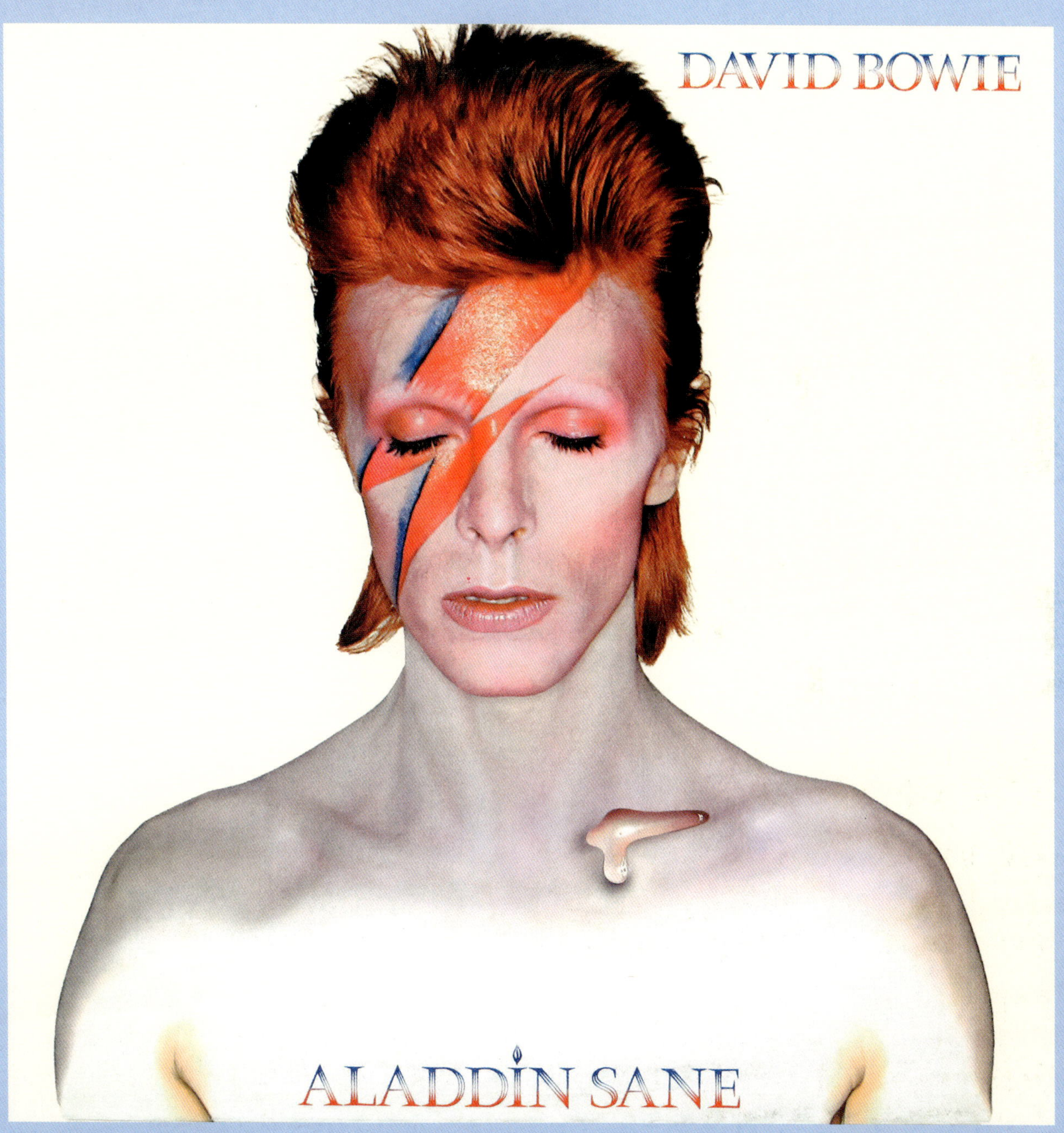

The photo by Brian Duffy for the iconic cover of Aladdin Sane, with the multicolored lightning bolt across the face. The tear inside Bowie's collarbone was added by artist Philip Castle, using an aerograph.

The songs on *Aladdin Sane* were written during that American tour, a journey made by train and Greyhound bus in the autumn of 1972.

This time, however, there is no distinctive style or theme to act as a common thread. "I don't think Aladdin is as clearly defined and specified as Ziggy," Bowie explained to the *New Musical Express* in 1973. "Aladdin is quite ephemeral. It's also one or more situations rather than a single individual." And his sound palette is also more complex, suspended between rock 'n' roll nostalgia, raw sounds à la the Stones, a theatrical dimension, and overseas sound suggestions: the avant-garde jazz of the syncopated title track (inspired by the satirical novel *Vile Bodies* by Evelyn Waugh) with Mike Garson's overflowing piano solo, the '50s doo-wop of *The Prettiest Star* and "Drive-In Saturday," the Hispanic scents of "Lady Grinning Soul," complete with a flamenco-style break by Ronson on the guitar.

"It was Ziggy meeting fame . . . the product of my paranoid relationship with America at the time. I wanted to be onstage singing my songs, but at the same time I didn't want to be on those buses with all those strange people," Bowie explained. So the man who would one day write "I'm Afraid of Americans" does not hide his mixture of disapproval and fascination for that reality, showing glimpses of degenerate lives, with violence, drug addicts, and gangsters alternating with dreamy Hollywood and science-fiction suggestions.

If the latter contributes to the album's sonic evolution, Ronson's guitar maintains continuity with Ziggy and the glam era, snarling with supersonic riffs worthy of Keith Richards's *Exile on Main Street* (and the homage to the Stones is precisely the cover of "Let's Spend the Night Together"). The critics were disoriented. The public, however, had no doubts and welcomed *Aladdin Sane* enthusiastically, sending it to first place in the UK Chart, where it stayed for five weeks, and, for the first time, in the Top 20 in the United States (at no. 17).

end," he will tell in "Moonage Daydream": "I was bored with the character of Ziggy Stardust. I couldn't concentrate on the performance anymore. . . . I was destroyed and sad."

On May 15, 1973, David Bowie departs from King's Cross Station in London, heading to Aberdeen, Scotland, for another leg of the Ziggy Stardust Tour.

So, when the tour resumed, Bowie contemplated that fateful exit, symbolic and dramatic. On the occasion of the final stop, on July 3, 1973, at the Hammersmith Odeon in London, he got rid of his cumbersome alter ego by making him "die" onstage and disbanding the Spiders from Mars. "This is not just the last concert of the tour, but also the last concert we will do. Goodbye. We love you," he said to the audience shortly before the encore of "Rock 'n' Roll Suicide," with many condolences to the fans, petrified and in tears. "It was a creature born to be idolized by the fans, I used it through the simple canons of rock 'n' roll," its executioner would conclude with pleased cynicism. From that historic show, director DA Pennebaker will make a concert film, shot in 16 mm, containing several sections of "behind the scenes" footage, in the dressing room and in the corridors of the theater.

But it is anything but a rock 'n' roll suicide. Soon, the glam epic will dissolve into the stardust of its hero. Thus the London *coup de théâtre* hides the foresight and pragmatism of an artist who, by killing the character who had given him the longed-for celebrity, knows how to grasp the intimate essence of the dynamics of the music business, which buries artists with the same speed with which it praises them. The philosophy of sudden changes aimed at keeping attention on himself will guide him in the years to come, until it transforms him into a shrewd self-manager. "The precise moment in which you feel safe, you're dead, you're finished," he will confide in 1976. "The last thing I want is to feel settled."

The mourning process for the death of Ziggy Stardust does not last more than a few days. Not satisfied with the glories of three spectacular albums churned out in a matter of two years (*Hunky Dory*, *Ziggy Stardust*, and *Aladdin Sane*), Bowie locks himself in the studio for a new project: the first collection of covers of his career. He is still supported—and for the last time before a long break—by his trusted Ronson, with what remains of the disbanded Spiders from Mars; namely, bassist Trevor Bolder, but only because the hoped-for replacement with ex-Cream Jack Bruce fails. Woodmansey is instead dismissed, and his place behind the drums is taken by Aynsley Dunbar. Keyboardist Mike Garson is added to the lineup.

1973

"The moment you feel safe, you're finished," Bowie claims. And so the mourning for Ziggy's death doesn't last more than a few days.

Left: David Bowie welcomed by his fans at the Hammersmith Odeon in London for the concert on July 3, 1973

Above: Adoring fans try to touch Bowie's hand during the historical show when he announced Ziggy Stardust's death.

The recordings took place in France, at the Chateau d' Hérouville, already immortalized by Elton John in an album from a year earlier (*Honky Chateau*). A month of highly tensed sessions, in which the only thing that weighs is not only the dismemberment of the Spiders from Mars, but also the beginning of Bowie's addiction to cocaine, which makes him increasingly unstable and authoritarian. The result, however, is a bizarre and surprising album, which combines the peculiar choice of repertoire with personal and captivating interpretations. "Pinups" is an eccentric tribute to the mod/beat roots, to the listening of the adolescent years in swinging London. Almost all the original songs are English, with the exception of "Here Comes the Night" by Them, led by Northern Irishman Van Morrison—transformed into a solemn ceremony punctuated by sax and guitars—and "Friday on My Mind" by the Australian Easybeats.

The Pinups cover is a quirky tribute to the teenage years in swinging London

The most-outstanding ones are the freer reinterpretations, in which Bowie infuses the grandeur of glam into the fabric of the songs, distorting them compared to the originals. Above all, the new "See Emily Play"—a psychedelic gem from the early Barrett-era Pink Floyd—no less alienating in its new orchestral setting, between strings and choirs, but also the combative "I Can't Explain" by the Who, remodeled into a warm and sensual soul ballad with sax, and a morbidly mellifluous "Sorrow," preferable even to the Merseys' version. More faithful to the originals, however, are the reinterpretations of other songs, such as "Rosalyn" by Pretty Things, the Yardbirds' double ("I Wish You Would" and "Shapes of Things"), and the other mod creature

The cover of Pinups*, with Bowie in a cerulean mask next to model Twiggy, in a photo by Justin de Villeneuve*

by the Who ("Anyway, Anyhow, Anywhere"), while the cover of "Where Have All the Good Times Gone" closes the set list with a nostalgia for the lost innocence of a British Arcadia.

On the cover, glamour still claims its share: Bowie is portrayed with the model Twiggy—already mentioned in "Drive-In Saturday" as "Twig the Wonder Kid"—in a shot by his manager and photographer Justin de Villeneuve. The two appear made up like cerulean masks, with enigmatic and alienating expressions.

Despite the clearly nostalgic nature of the operation and the lukewarm reaction of the critics, *Pinups* flew to the top of the UK Chart for five weeks. Curiously, however, the most famous Bowie cover of the period did not end up in his track list but is included as the B side of the single "Sorrow," released in parallel: a poignant revisitation of Jacques Brel's Amsterdam.

Gratified by his successes but pursued by his demons, Bowie enters a spiral of uncertainty and chaos, without, however, losing his ambition to experiment with new artistic hybrids. Returning to London from Japan, he travels for a week on the Trans-Siberian line, being impressed by Soviet totalitarianism and the control it exercises over the population. Thus, the idea of a show centered on George Orwell's *1984* matures, which had already struck him at the time of the song "Cygnet Committee" (1969) with the reference to the sad story of the protagonists of the novel, Winston and Julia: "And I close my eyes and tighten up my brain / For I once read a book where lovers were slain / For they knew not the words of the Free States' refrain."

The vision of a dehumanizing and alienated world, subjugated by totalitarianism, is a recurring obsession in his work. "Dystopia has been a strong theme in the work I've done over the years," he explained to *Mojo* magazine in 2002. "I think the apocalyptic vision can be seen as the manifestation of an internal problem."

The artwork by Belgian artist Guy Peellaert for the cover of Diamond Dogs, *in which Bowie turns into a monstrous creature, half man, half dog, striking a pose that recalls a photo by Josephine Baker. With him are two disturbing female figures inspired by Alzoria Lewis and Johanna Dickens, who were among the protagonists of the* Cavalcade Variety Show.

The dream of a theatrical transposition of *1984* into a musical, however, has to deal with the firm opposition of Orwell's widow, Sonia, who denies the rights. And so, as with Ziggy Stardust, from the idea of a musical a concept album is born. It's titled *Diamond Dogs* and is immortalized by a disconcerting artwork signed by the Belgian artist Guy Peellaert, in which Bowie transforms into a monstrous being, half man, half dog, taking a pose that recalls a photo of Josephine Baker taken in 1926; with him are two disturbing female figures inspired by Alzoria Lewis and Johanna Dickens, among the protagonists of the bizarre *Cavalcade Variety Show*, staged at the Coney Island Pleasure Park between the 1930s and 1950s.

The recordings take place between the London-based Olympic Studios and Ludolf Nederhorst Studios of Berg, in Holland, where the Rolling Stones were recording the album *It's Only Rock 'n' Roll*. A climate of permanent instability

In addition to the disintegration of the Spiders from Mars, there is also the end of the experience with the producer Ken Scott, who will shortly sit at the console of Supertramp for one of their masterpieces, *Crime of the Century*. Bowie decides to produce the album himself, with the help of the sound engineer Keith Harwood, and calling back his friend Tony Visconti: He was returning after a four-year hiatus and destined to remain one of the (few) certainties of the period, helping Bowie for the entire decade. Orphaned of his counterpart Ronson, the former Ziggy Stardust takes up the guitar and juggles the sax, Moog, and Mellotron, recruiting Herbie Flowers on bass, Tony Newman (already in the Jeff Beck Group) and Aynsley Dunbar alternating on drums, and Garson on keyboards.

Besides *1984*, the most direct source of inspiration is the apocalyptic urban vision of the novel *Wild Boys* by William Burroughs. Always attracted by his work, Bowie had the opportunity to meet the legendary beat writer on November 17, 1973, for a long conversation, from which a double interview was taken, published in *Rolling Stone* the following February with the title "Beat Godfather Meets Glitter Mainman." On that occasion, the English artist said he was particularly struck by Burroughs's use of the "cut-up," a technique inspired by Dadaism, which consists of physically cutting a written text, leaving only some of the words and sentences intact, then mixing the various fragments and thus recomposing a new text, an influence that will remain a constant in Bowie's entire songwriting.

Marrying these literary inspirations with a new infatuation with German expressionist cinema instigated by his friend Amanda Lear, who had taken him to see Fritz Lang's *Metropolis* at a Hampstead cinema, Bowie predicted the advent of the Diamond Dogs, feral kids living on the roofs of skyscrapers and terrorizing anyone who wandered the streets of a desolate Manhattan, transformed into "Hunger City."

But the backbone remains the dystopian novel by Orwell, to whom the album's leading song is dedicated. Originally born in a medley ("1984/Dodo"), the result of the last session in the company of Ronson and Scott and anticipated on TV at *The 1980 Floor Show*, "1984" introduces the musical turning point of the entire album: a mix between the majesty of glam rock and those soul and funk suggestions of the "Philly Sound" that Bowie would then convincingly embrace in the following LP, *Young Americans*. Framed by Visconti in a solemn string orchestration and punctuated by the crackling sound of a guitar filtered with wah-wah (cured by Alan Parker), the song highlights one of the most melodramatic interpretations of Bowie, a menacing crooner on the brink of the abyss of a humanity destined to brutal psychological degradation: "They'll split your pretty skull and fill it full of air."

A theatrical approach, from an afterlife Brel, which becomes even more spectacular in the three-part suite "Sweet Thing"–"Candidate"–"Sweet Thing (Reprise)," with a performance that can range with ease from sepulchral bass to high falsetto notes with a full throat. A vocal imprinting inspired by Scott Walker's crooning, which Bowie introduces for the first time on this album, and which will increasingly characterize his following works. The nine-minute sequence features a massive use of cutups, at the service of crude snapshots of depravity and urban decadence, with disturbing figures such as Charles Manson and *les tricoteuses*, the women who knitted at the foot of the guillotine during the French Revolution. A portrait in flesh of a dehumanized society, where sex is experienced as a self-destructive drug consumption. Up to the desperate conclusion of "Candidate": "We'll buy some drugs and listen to a band play and jump in the river holding hands." With piano chimes, sax swirls, and distorted rock guitar rumblings, Bowie celebrates the requiem of an entire generation, laying bare all the specters of the drug addiction that is beginning to grip him.

Obsessed by the Orwellian Big Brother of *1984*, Bowie narrates a dystopian world adrift among sex, drugs, and omens of death.

In this rotten and crumbling world, subjugated to Big Brother, the only possible redemption is the hopeless love of "We Are the Dead," another Orwellian homage inspired by the dialogue between the protagonists of *1984*, Winston and Julia, who repeat this very phrase to each other ("We are the dead") shortly before the Thought Police arrive to arrest them. Embellished with guitar feedback, electric piano, and melodramatic crooning, it is a little gem that will remain under the radar in the London artist's repertoire, perhaps because it's never been performed live.

David Bowie onstage at the last live appearance of Ziggy Stardust, at the Hammersmith Odeon in London, July 3, 1973

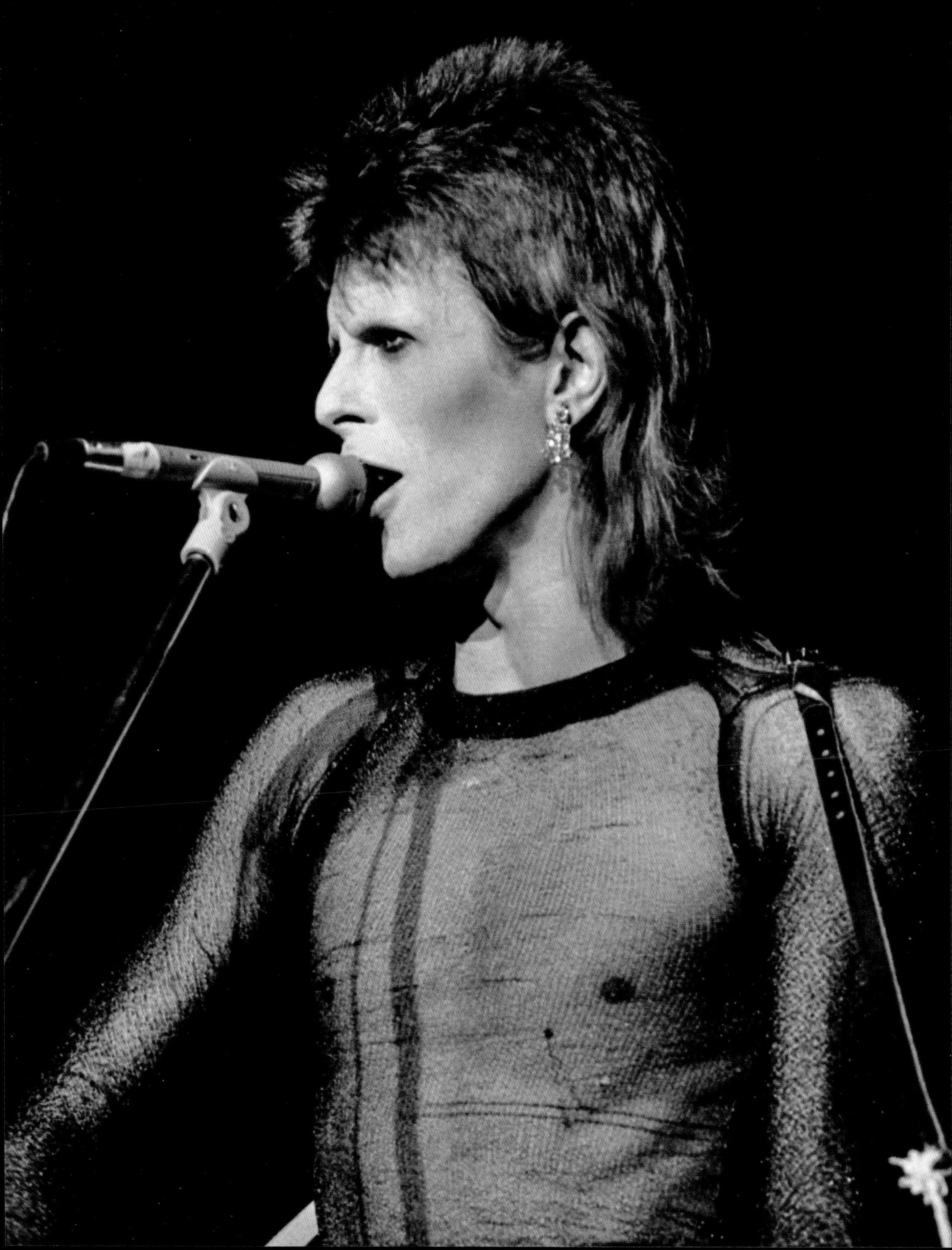

But Bowie has not lost his perk for masks. The former Ziggy Stardust is thus reincarnated in a new (ephemeral) character named Halloween Jack, "a real cool cat," who lives on the roof of the Manhattan Chase in the urban desolation of Hunger City, leading the Diamond Dogs gangs from his hideout. A new look will also be created for the shows: increasingly bright-red hair, pirate eye patch, protopunk outfit, and a more angular approach, like a survivor of the postapocalyptic urban desert. The title track introduces him with a disconcerting touch: "This ain't rock 'n' roll—this is genocide!" The idea of street gangs, instead, comes from a synthesis of various literary sources: William Burroughs's *The Wild Boys*, but also the Droogs in *A Clockwork Orange* by Anthony Burgess (transposed to the big screen by Kubrick) and Charles Dickens's stray kids. "They were toothless and dirty, a sort of violent Oliver Twist," imagines Bowie, also influenced by the stories told by his father, who worked for Dr. Barnardo's Children Home, a charity for underprivileged children. "It was an extraordinary image, which stayed in my mind, all those kids who lived on the roofs of London," he will say. "So here were my Diamond Dogs living on the streets. They were all little Johnny Rottens and Sid Viciouses . . . they were precursors of punk." This is to reiterate how in the Bowie visions of the '70s there was already more than one germ of the movement that would soon infect England, under the leadership of the Sex Pistols, the Clash, Buzzcocks, etc.

The album's anthem will paradoxically become the song most alien to the leaden apocalyptic climate that pervades it: "Rebel Rebel," with its sticky Stones-style riff, once again paying off the debt to Keith Richards, Mick Jagger & Co.

Defined by Bowie as "my first album entirely recorded under the influence of cocaine," *Diamond Dogs* is a work as fascinating as it is chaotic and, in some ways, unfinished, which, as usual, will divide the critics but will still seduce the public (no. 1 in the UK and no. 5 in the USA). It will find its ideal dimension onstage, in an astonishing tour, designed by Jules Fisher and Mark Ravitz, with ambitious sets, borrowed from German expressionism (with explicit references to the painting of George Grosz, the films *Metropolis* by Fritz Lang and *Das Cabinet des Dr. Caligari* by Robert Wiene). In the apocalyptic scenario of Hunger City, among ruined skyscrapers and spaceships, limping dog-men and other scattered wrecks of humanity toil, while Bowie towers from the top of a crane, recites, mimes, and often changes his look, like an experienced stage actor. His glittering makeup also features a small circle of sequins on his forehead. A sort of futuristic third eye.

David Bowie performs with a patch on his eye for the Dutch show TopPop *in February 1974.*

同春

IN HIS LIVE SHOWS, BOWIE SINGS, ACTS, MIMES, AND OFTEN CHANGES HIS LOOK, LIKE A VETERAN THEATER ACTOR

Previous pages and left: David Bowie onstage at the Earls Court Arena in London, May 12, 1973, during the Ziggy Stardust tour

Above: During the same show, he mimes the famous sexual act on Spiders from Mars's Mick Ronson's guitar.

In the evenings of July 14 and 15, 1974, of the Diamond Dogs Tour at the Tower Theater in Philadelphia, the double *David Live* will be recorded, whose famous cover portrays an emaciated and vampiric Bowie, now dressed more as a night cabaret soulman than as a glam star: It is no coincidence that a hymn to the glitter season like "All the Young Dudes" is part of the set list in an unprecedented soul guise, and arrangements emerge winking at Black music, which is also recalled with the cover of a classic like "Knock on Wood" by Eddie Floyd. The sound output of the performances, however, is poor, to the despair of producer Tony Visconti, who at the time came to define *David Live as* "one of the most rushed and shoddy albums I have ever made." Thanks to modern technologies, however, he will be able to redeem it through a new version (2005 mix / 2016 remaster), significantly improving the sound quality.

David Live photographs the American tour, with the latest glam notes and the first seeds of the soul era

First live album of Bowie's discography, *David Live* remains in any case the document of a crucial period of transition, containing within itself the last fragrances of the glam era and at the same time the first seeds of that sensational soul-turning point that would bury "rock 'n' roll with lipstick" forever.

Left: David Bowie onstage during his Ziggy Stardust Tour at the Long Beach Arena, California, 1973

Above: The cover of his first live LP, David Live *(1974), part of the the* Diamond Dogs *Tour at the Tower Theatre in Philadelphia, July 14 and 15, 1974*

3

FROM LOS ANGELES TO BERLIN, IN SEARCH OF SALVATION

THE GHOSTS DISSOLVE IN THE SHADOW OF THE WALL: THE REBIRTH OF THE THIN WHITE DUKE

David Bowie's infatuation with Black American music did not come suddenly. Among his listening habits as a teenager, American blues and R&B occupied a significant portion of his time. And if Little Richard was one of his idols, it was the program *Soul Train*—where he would later be among the first white artists to perform—that he had an authentic veneration for. "It was obvious that sooner or later he would make an R&B record," says Tony Visconti, who would also support this evolution as a producer. After all, *Aladdin Sane* was already Ziggy's travel diary in America, while the concerts overseas had strengthened the bond with the United States and with their deepest musical soul, through a progressive mutation of the arrangements and set lists. So if in *David Live*—documenting the first leg of the Diamond Dogs Tour—one could already glimpse the signs of a transformation, in the second leg—the Philly Dogs Tour—the metamorphosis is complete. This brought repercussions also on the composition of the band: a new formidable guitarist with a soul-R&B background, Carlos Alomar, joins Earl Slick, the amazing singer Luther Vandross on backing vocals, and a rhythm section centered on Doug Rauch on bass and Greg Errico on drums, in addition to David Sanborn (wind instruments) and the trusted Garson (keyboards). Thanks also to

The newly added band member, guitarist Carlos Alomar, helps generate the new sound of "Young Americans"

this new lineup, which would later also include Willie Weeks and drummer Dennis Davis, Bowie staged a real Black celebration, with obvious tributes (the covers of the aforementioned "Knock on Wood," "Here Today and Gone Tomorrow" by the Ohio Players, and "Footstompin" by the Flares), new arrangements of old songs that already bore the signs of a turning point ("Rock 'n' Roll with Me," 1984) and some appetizers from the sessions of the new LP in progress, such as "It's Gonna Be Me" and the soul remake of his 45 rpm from 1972, "John, I'm Only Dancing" (both later excluded from the track list). During a break in the tour, David locks himself in the studio in Philadelphia, the cradle of the so-called Philly Sound, a genre of soul derivation, with funk, R&B, and jazz influences. It is the dawn of a new revolution: the era of Young Americans. But nothing happens by chance in Bowie's quick-change workshop. "I thought I had to make a successful album to consolidate my position in the US; I made up my mind, and I did it. It wasn't difficult," he confided to *Melody Maker*. So after Ziggy, the glamorous Bowie is also buried, to make room for a dandy who has lost his platform shoes, sequins, and a lot of mascara along the way but has retained an ambiguous and disturbing look. The new frontier is therefore the America of funk, R&B, and dawning disco music. An America that has lost the sinister connotations described in *Aladdin Sane* and *Hunky Dory*, returning to embody "the land of a thousand dances." The manifesto of this "plastic soul" hybrid is the title track, "Young Americans," a pressing pop anthem that unfolds on disco pulses, between piano and sax, supported by festive backing vocals. With gospel-like lyrics that review the vices and virtues of twentieth-century America, including references to the Watergate scandal ("Do you remember, your President Nixon?"), Senator McCarthy's witch hunt ("Now you've become the anti-American"), and a well-known episode in the struggle for Black civil rights ("You're standing idly on a survivors' bus, blushing at the sight of all the black shoeshine boys"), citing icons of American consumerism ("Ford Mustang," "Barbie Doll," "Chrysler") in a foretaste of the future *I'm Afraid of Americans* twenty years later. The work at Sigma Sound Studios, under the direction of Visconti, has a primary objective: to make the atmosphere of the songs as immediate as possible, as if they had been recorded live in a single session.

The new team of musicians is joined by Andy Newmark, drummer of a funk institution like Sly & the Family Stone, who in the '80s will put himself at the service of the languid sound tinged with black of Roxy Music's *Flesh and Blood* and *Avalon*.

The result is a powerful soul machine in which the beacon is Alomar, former member of James Brown's group, with his arsenal of lightning-fast riffs. Dazzled by Bowie's talent, by whose side he would remain for a long time, becoming the most present musician in his albums, the Puerto Rican guitarist was also impressed by his evident state of alteration, due to cocaine abuse: "He was the whitest man I had ever seen: Practically translucent and with orange hair, he weighed no more than 45 kilos," he would later say.

Despite this, Bowie appears to be in good vocal shape, refining his style in a Black key. In an ideal cross between Abbey Road and Harlem, he creates tributes to jazz fusion such as "Win" and "Right," funk grooves with a quick catch ("Fascination"), and soul longings inspired by Aretha Franklin and Marvin Gaye ("Can You Hear Me"). But what makes the album historic in its own way—even beyond its intrinsic value—is the stellar meeting between David Bowie and John Lennon. The two met in New York, where the ex-Beatle was consummating his famous lost weekend, the period of excess spent away from Yoko Ono. And they decide to try a session together at Electric Lady Studios, recording a cover of the Beatles' "Across the Universe." But the main hit is a new song, reworked starting from the guitar riff that Alomar had conceived for the cover of "Footstompin'." John and David have dinner together, and when they return to the studio, the song has already come to life through Alomar's fingers; Bowie adds a small guitar part and the lyrics, to be punctuated in a sort of metallic protorap. The result is "Fame," a funky-beat meditation on the fleeting nature of success: "Fame, it puts you where things are false / Fame, it ain't your brain, it's just the flame / That burns your change to keep you crazy . . . / Fame, what you get is no tomorrow / Fame, what you need you gotta borrow." Not exactly the sum of the two authors' immense talents, but the right song to disrupt the US charts: It will be Bowie's first single to rise to no. 1 and will drive the entire LP *Young Americans*. "I was excited to work with John, and he loved being with my band because we played old soul songs and Stax-style stuff. John had a special energy," David will remember. Visconti will not be present at the production stages of the songs with Lennon, who will have the opportunity to mitigate his regret by meeting his future wife, May Pang, who had been the partner of the former Beatle.

Perhaps even more than the artistic aspect, however, Bowie's management will benefit from the meeting with Lennon. John will push David to break the ties with Tony Defries, who had left him with a huge debt. From here a legal proceeding, entrusted to the lawyer Michael Lippman, closed with an agreement—considered not too favorable to Bowie—which foresaw the possibility of obtaining full rights to the new songs only from September 30, 1982, the expiration date of the contract with Defries.

David Bowie and John Lennon during the seventeenth edition of the Grammy Awards at the Uris Theater in New York City, March 1, 1975

An artificial portrait of a soul man—starting from the cover, with a heavily airbrushed photo of Eric Stephen Jacobs—*Young Americans* split critics and disoriented fans. While some will call it "the first Black soul album recorded by a white musician," there will be no shortage of detractors, ready to point out its nature as a cold exercise in style. The author himself, however, will not be tender toward it: "I don't listen to it often. I don't like it very much. It was just a phase," he revealed in 1976 to *Melody Maker*. Only to soften his judgment later, in an interview with *Q* in 1990: "At the time, I expressed myself without any emotional involvement. But in retrospect that album was a decent example of blue-eyed soul."

BOWIE MOVES TO LOS ANGELES, WHERE HE SINKS INTO A METROPOLITAN NIGHTMARE, BETWEEN PARANOIA AND DRUG ADDICTION

In any case, Bowie was once again ahead of his time, breaking down further barriers between genres: Soon after, droves of white artists would jump on the disco bandwagon, starting with the Bee Gees infected by *Saturday Night Fever*. But of course when the disco craze exploded, Bowie was already somewhere else. Not physically, though. Because, attracted by the sirens of show business and cinema, in which he had debuted with the film *The Man Who Fell to Earth* (1976), he settled in Los Angeles, where one of the darkest periods of his existence would begin.

North Doheny Drive, Bel Air, a stone's throw from the villa where in 1969 the bloodthirsty followers of Charles Manson's sect killed five people, including actress Sharon Tate, wife of director Roman Polanski: Here the future Thin White Duke sinks into full narcotic chaos. His marriage is in tatters, relationships with his managers are stormy, and his existence seems on the verge of imploding.

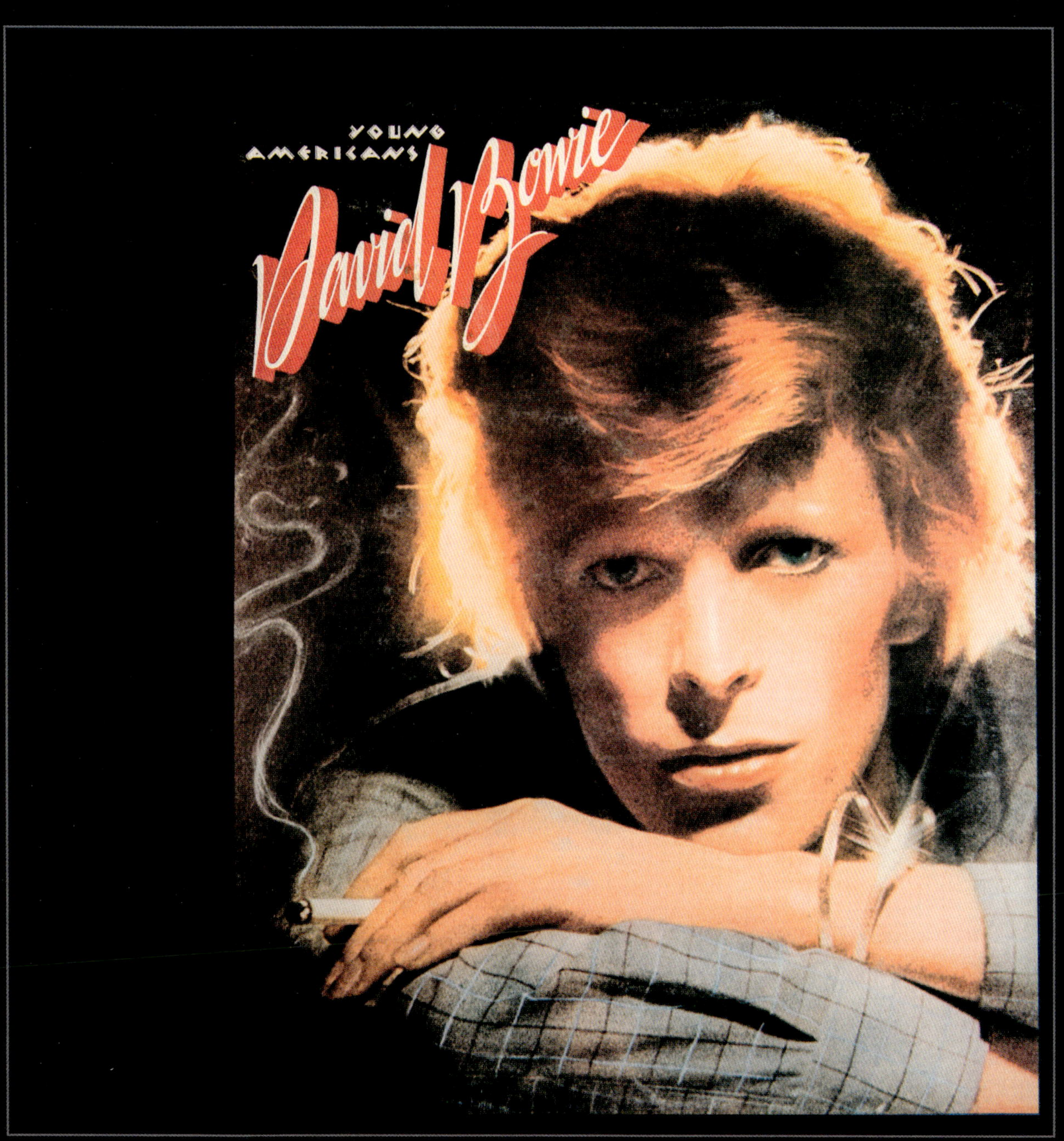

1975

David Bowie with a new look, photographed by Eric Stephen Jacobs for the cover of Young Americans (1975), the album of his "plastic soul" era

Gaunt, emaciated, like the metropolitan vampire in the film *Miriam Wakes Up at Midnight* that he would play a few years later, he retreats to his apartment, prey to his phobias.

The Los Angeles–era David Bowie took excessive amounts of cocaine and lived on a diet of cigarettes, chili peppers, and milk, spending the two-year period from 1975 through 1976 in a state of constant psychotic terror. Contemporaneous accounts—mostly from an interview with reporter Cameron Crowe, appeared in *Playboy* and *Rolling Stone* magazines—describe Bowie living in an apartment filled with ancient Egyptian artifacts and constantly burning black candles, surrounded by Nazi iconography, studying black-magic treatises and storing his own bottled urine in the fridge, terrified that a group of witches wanted to steal his sperm for some dark ritual, and eventually receiving secret messages from the Rolling Stones and threats from Led Zeppelin's Jimmy Page (a notorious follower of Aleister Crowley). He himself recalled that dramatic period: "I weighed less than 100 pounds. It was really painful. I was paranoid, manic depressive: the usual emotional side effect that comes with abusing amphetamines, cocaine, and all the rest."

David Bowie posing for a photo portrait in 1976

But it was precisely during those Californian days, in delirious sessions between rivers of cocaine ("I know they were held in Los Angeles because I read about it," he would later confide), that he would create an innovative album titled *Station to Station* (1976), which would bring him back into the charts (no. 3 in the USA, no. 5 in the UK), inaugurating another extraordinary musical season.

The aristocratic Thin White Duke is born, a cold and alienated character, on whom Bowie will pour all the obsessions of the period.

As often happens, however, the London artist feels the need to split himself in two, to identify an alter ego on which to place his burden of suffering and sick fantasies. For the occasion, a new character forms, destined to become his most famous alias. His name is in a verse of the title track, which was also the one initially chosen to give the title to the album: *The Return of the Thin White Duke*. Red-blond hair slicked back, white waistcoat and shirt, black pleated trousers, the Thin White Duke is a cold and aristocratic being, intoxicated by drugs, alienated by urban paranoia, and isolated in his world of robotic music, a close relative of the character of Thomas Newton played by Bowie in the film *The Man Who Fell to Earth*. On him, he will vent all the obsessions of the period, including an unhealthful attraction to Nazi mythology. "The Thin White Duke was a rather hateful being, an ogre. But ultimately the best way to fight an evil force is to reduce it to a caricature," he would theorize a few years later.

For the studio sessions in October 1975, Bowie gathered a large group of musicians: Carlos Alomar, Earl Slick, Dennis Davis, Warren Peace, George Murray, and Roy Bittan (a pianist in Bruce Springsteen's circle), thus laying the foundations for the Murray-Davis-Alomar rhythm section that would play on all his subsequent LPs up to 1980's *Scary Monsters*. Recorded at Cherokee and Record Plant Studios in Los Angeles, *Station to Station* is the fruit of complete artistic freedom. While the hybrid plastic soul of *Young Americans* remained a formal abstraction, the new songs hit the mark, blending guitar rock with electronics and the warm and primitive beat of Black music with the icy synths of the Germans Kraftwerk and Neu! (on the California freeways, Bowie traveled with *Autobahn* as a soundtrack, dreaming of returning to "his" Europe).

the synthetic sound of a locomotive, Slick's guitar riffs, and a few sparse synth phrases, before the entrance of the Thin White Duke and the dizzying final crescendo, in which Bowie confirms himself as an extraordinarily histrionic interpreter. If possible, the live version included in *Stage*, the 1978 live album, will be even better.

Influenced by Kraftwerk, Bowie will end up seducing the Teutonic quartet, who the following year in the definitive suite *Trans-Europe Express* will recite, "From station to station, back to Düsseldorf city, meet Iggy Pop and David Bowie." The game of cross-references, continued with V-2 Schneider in "Heroes," will be so dazzling that it will infect the new-wave generations (Ultravox, Simple Minds, Depeche Mode, OMD, and others), who will have in the Bowie-Kraftwerk duo their protective gods.

With his mind projected into the future, the Thin White Duke writes cryptic lyrics, inspired by cybernetics and fantasy television systems, taken to the extreme in "TVC 15": a vintage piano opens the curtain on a game of guitar and synth-pop keyboards, spiced up by delirious vocalizations (the "oh oh oh oh oh" repeated twenty-eight times!). "Golden Years" is instead the single that was for the western film of the same name a year later, which will become a classic by Black icon Nina Simone: Between acoustic guitars and soft keyboards, Bowie intensifies its epic and poignant dimension with an acrobatic vocal number, accentuating that deep crooner tone destined to remain one of his traits.

A dark album, imbued with occult and disturbing symbolism, with numerous references to black magic, the Jewish Kabbalah, and the Tree of Life, *Station to Station* is the testimony of Bowie's peculiar American "via crucis." "It had a certain magnetism, which is usually associated with magic," he said in 1999. "The words 'station to station' themselves have a meaning if they refer to the stations of the Via Crucis, but I went further: They referred to the kabbalistic Tree of Life."

The cover of Station to Station *(1976), which was a still from the film* The Man Who Fell to Earth, *where Bowie, as the alien Thomas Jerome Newton, enters an anechoic chamber.*

1976

The next tour abandons the excesses of the past, with bare sets, illuminated by cold white neon lights, on which images are projected from the film *Un Chien Andalou (An Andalusian Dog)* by Luis Buñuel and Salvador Dalí. "A synthesis between Bertolt Brecht and the Doors," as Bowie defines it, who renews the homage to Kraftwerk, using their music before his entrance onstage, and hosts onstage Iggy Pop, just released from the Institute of Mental Hygiene. Destroyed by the American adventure, the two former "chemical brothers" will meet again in Europe, where a new life will begin for both.

The California nightmare officially comes to an end during the aborted sessions for the soundtrack of *The Man Who Fell to Earth*. One day, overwhelmed by stress, Bowie collapses on the floor in the studio. He decides to make a radical change in his life: He fires Lippman, who had temporarily replaced Defries as his manager, gives up the soundtrack, which will be entrusted to John Phillips of the Mamas and the Papas, and plans to leave Los Angeles immediately.

The Californian nightmare is over: Bowie and his friend Iggy Pop will meet again in Berlin, where a new life will begin for both of them.

Bowie performs as the Thin White Duke during a leg of his Station to Station World Tour at the Wembley Empire Pool in London, May 1976.

1976

Above: Bowie as theThin White Duke, during the show at the Wembley Empire Pool

Right: Bowie during a show of the Station to Station Tour at the Falkoner in Copenaghen, Denmark, April 29, 1976

COMPAGNIE
HYATT HOTELS

At the end of the tour, after a brief interlude in Switzerland, Bowie moved with his assistant Coco Schwab and Iggy Pop to Berlin. Exhausted by Los Angeles, which he would come to define as "the most repulsive boil of the scum of humanity," he felt the call of the Old Continent, of that mother culture in many ways opposed to the American one, which almost devoured him. It was something he understood definitively during the Station to Station tour, when in the company of Iggy Pop he found himself crossing eastern Europe by train. The city of the Berlin Wall, a lacerating symbol of the Cold War, but also the cradle of central Europe, with its leaden decadent malady, played as an irresistible attraction. The electronic music scene; the expressionist cinema of Fritz Lang, Friedrich Wilhelm Murnau, and Georg Wilhelm Pabst; the Brechtian cabaret; and the new German painting movement fascinated the former restless boy from Brixton. "Since my adolescence, I had been obsessed with the emotional and angst-filled work of the expressionist artists, and Berlin had been their spiritual home," he explained in 1978. "This was the center of the Die Brücke movement, of Max Reinhardt and Bertolt Brecht; this was where *Metropolis* and *The Cabinet of Dr. Caligari* were born. It was an art form that reflected life not through the event, but through the state of mind. This is the direction I felt my work was going."

Left: David Bowie and Iggy Pop at the central station in Copenaghen, 1976
Above: The two friends in Germany in 1977

Bowie sees in the city of the Berlin Wall "the center of everything that is happening and that will happen in the coming years in Europe," the ideal place to "discover new forms of writing and develop a new musical language." And this is exactly what he will be able to achieve with the famous trilogy *Low-"Heroes"-Lodger*, the result of the collaboration with Brian Eno. The guru of ambient music had met Bowie in the spring of 1976 in Wembley, during a stop on the Station to Station Tour, and had been struck by the connotations that the ex-Ziggy's music had taken on. Bowie himself had already begun working on instrumental tracks conceived for the soundtrack of *The Man Who Fell to Earth* in 1975, using a compositional approach similar to that of Kraftwerk and Eno himself. It is no coincidence, therefore, that one of the most famous partnerships in the history of rock was born.

But first, the former Ziggy Stardust had to deal with a sensational scandal. On May 2, 1976, he arrived at Victoria Station in London. Photographer Chalkie Davies immortalized him aboard a Mercedes convertible while greeting fans with his left arm stretched in the air, in what was mistaken for a Nazi salute. "Unfortunately, because of the dark light, I had to use the flash," Davies later said. "I showed the image to NME, and they decided to retouch the arm by adding a hand, as it was partially missing because of the flash. When we then saw the newspaper, it looked like he was doing a Nazi salute."

The photo sparked the so-called Victoria Station incident. The reaction in England was furious. Bowie himself was disgusted by the use of the image: "I'm not a fascist," he swore to the press in 1977. "I was just waving." Moreover, by immersing himself in the reality of Berlin, he fully understood the ruin caused by Nazi fascism, developing a total rejection of racism and nationalism and defining his past interests as the aberrant fruit of a period of excess: "I was out of my mind; I was going crazy." Then he will add: "In Berlin I met these boys of my age who had had fathers in the SS, and it was a good way to wake up from the nightmare. Yes, returning to Europe was like falling back to Earth."

Determined to detox and revitalize his career, Bowie also had to deal with the dissolution of his marriage to Angela Barnett, which had been in crisis since 1973 and was now heading toward the end. It would end up in a divorce in 1980. After a few sporadic visits to Berlin, Angie broke off relations following David's refusal to fire Coco Schwab, of whom she was uncontrollably jealous.

Left: David Bowie with Robert Fripp and Brian Eno at the Hansa Tonstudio in Berlin, 1977

Above: The famous photo of the "Victoria Station Incident," May 2, 1976

But it is once again in music that Bowie finds his main creative therapy, chasing away those ghosts that were now threatening his very survival. "I was about to become the protagonist of yet another death in the world of rock," he will say in 1996. "I would not have survived the seventies if I had continued to do what I was doing. I was lucky enough to feel somewhere inside me that I was killing myself and that I had to do something drastic to get out of all this."

The way out is an album with an austere and minimalist approach, destined to remain among the most important of his entire career. "It's what I wanted to do for the soundtrack of *The Man Who Fell to Earth,"* Bowie will write in a letter to director Nicolas Roeg, increasing his regrets for that collaboration that did not end well. Instead, the snapshot of a new, surprising Bowian palingenesis will emerge: *Low*, as in the low profile needed to reinvent himself again.

Neither Brian Eno nor the Berlin studios, however, play a less relevant role in this first chapter of the trilogy. By the time the sessions were well underway, the pioneer of ambient music contributed more as a sound supervisor than as an active member of Bowie's team (with the exception of "Warszawa"), beginning to introduce compositional techniques that would find expression in subsequent works, such as the use of Oblique Strategies, a set of cards containing cryptic instructions such as "Fill each bar with something" or "Use an acceptable color," aimed at helping the musicians break down mental blocks. More significant was the contribution of producer Visconti, who was responsible, among other things, for the sound experiments with percussion through a new type of device, the Harmonizer Eventide, a protosampler that captured, modified, and simultaneously returned sounds, giving the drums new timbres. The main recording location was not the German metropolis, but the Château d'Hérouville, near Paris, an ancient castle converted into a studio, where Bowie had already recorded *Pinups* and had just finished working on Iggy Pop's *The Idiot*, the obscure protowave work destined to go down in history as the tragic soundtrack to the suicide of Ian Curtis of Joy Division. Only the sessions with the two final tracks ("Weeping Wall" and "Art Decade") were completed in Berlin, at the famous Hansa Studios, before the mixing began. The city of the Berlin Wall takes on the role of an ideal setting in the album, capable of inspiring its decadent feeling. The second side of the work, in particular, will be a sort of musical commentary on the atmospheres of the German metropolis split by the Iron Curtain of the Cold War.

David Bowie in his living room, London, late 1970s

Surrounded by a group of trusted musicians (in addition to Eno, grappling with synthesizers and treated guitars, Carlos Alomar on guitar, Dennis Davis on drums, Ricky Gardiner on guitar, George Murray on bass, Roy Young on piano and organ), the Thin White Duke conceives a work—initially titled *New Music, Night and Day*—devoted to experimentation, with the German luminaries of electronics—Kraftwerk, Neu!, and Tangerine Dream—and ambient music itself as crucial references. And yet, *Low* will achieve a notable commercial success, reaching no. 2 in the UK Chart and no. 11 in the *Billboard* Pop Albums chart in the US. This is mainly due to some of the tracks on the first side being more oriented toward the song format, in which the glacial atmospheres of kraut rock are combined with the warmth of R&B brought as a dowry by the consolidated rhythm section Alomar-Murray-Davis.

Influenced by Kraftwerk and kraut rock, Bowie conceives futuristic fragments as precursors of the new wave

There is foreshadowing of futuristic and schizoid fragments of new wave, such as the fading instrumental "Speed of Life," with Bowie on synths, the distorted snare drum, and the electric guitar blasts; the threatening electro-funk-rock of *Breaking Glass*, the story of a lover who destroys his woman's room, perhaps to sublimate the anger arising from the end of his marriage to Angela; the claustrophobic "What in the World," with its frantic pace marking an ode to the sense of isolation (vocals by Iggy Pop); and the disarming cry for help of "Be My Wife," with cascading piano and layers of keyboards pierced by guitar feedback. Plus two anthology-worthy tracks, "Sound and Vision" and "Always Crashing in the Same Car," which could ideally be added to the Bowie procession of *Station to Station*. In the first, behind the techno-pop rhythms of the treated drums, cocktail-lounge sax, and cascades of synthesizers, Bowie hides a reflection on alienation and personal failure, played on the ambiguity of the term "blue," to evoke the sadness of depression but also the awareness of the complicated path undertaken ("Blue, blue, electric blue / that's the color of my room / where I will live"), using the image of the room as a hideaway. Just like what will happen to the protagonist of *The Man Who Fell to Earth*, who will find himself alone in a room full of blue light coming from an entire wall of televisions. The second song, marked by Gardiner's feverish filtered guitar, offers instead the most powerful metaphor of the extreme existential condition that its author had reached: "Always Crashing in the Same Car." The reference is, however, to a real episode that occurred to Bowie, when, while driving under the influence of alcohol, he wasn't able to park his Mercedes in the hotel parking area, repeatedly hitting other cars.

The instrumental piece that closes the first side ("A New Career in a New Town") sounds like a tribute to the new life in Berlin and, at the same time, a prelude to the electronic experimentation that dominates side 2, in the name of twilight ambient music. The backbone of this second part is the six-minute-plus "Warszawa," written by Eno, who was asked to write "a very slow piece" capable of unleashing "an almost religious feeling." The dark synthesizers of the "nonmusician" are contrasted by Bowie's wordless singing, a Gregorian chant inspired by a choir of Bulgarian boys that he had had the opportunity to listen to: from ambient to world music in a single track, an experiment born as an attempt to capture the sense of desolation felt by David when visiting the city in 1976. Annihilated by the Nazis during the Second World War, the Polish capital embodied the anguish of the Cold War, with the looming specter of Soviet imperialism against which a few years later the Solidarność trade union revolt by Lech Walesa would be unleashed (1980), triggering the process of implosion of the entire Communist bloc in Europe. Bowie also tries to capture the religious spirit of a people who only two years later would offer the first Slavic pope in history, John Paul II. "Warszawa" will become a fetish song of the entire new wave. It is no coincidence that, in its honor, Joy Division will initially choose the name "Warsaw." But its shadow will continue to cast itself on future generations: "That album and that piece, 'Warszawa': that was the moment I understood that music was the greatest force in my life," confided Dave Sitek of TV on the Radio, an American band formed in 2001 that would later have the opportunity to collaborate with Bowie.

The final trio, on the other hand, is entirely of Berlin origin. "Art Decade" celebrates West Berlin, which the Iron Curtain cut off "from the world, from its art, from its culture," in the words of Bowie, who paints it by letting the synths float in a network of noisy drones and entrusting the sound engineer Eduard Meyer with a splendid cello line. It's a sorrowful vision of the disintegrated city, in which the Berlin Wall itself is crying: "Weeping Wall," a song still without words, between anxiety-inducing sounds and the ticking of Chinese chopsticks on a sinister backdrop of synths, distorted guitars, and choirs. "Subterraneans" closes the trio, with humble sax embroidery on an electronic base: It is the soundtrack of postdivision East Berlin, where "there were only jazz saxophones to represent the memory of what was," its author will explain.

Accompanied by another memorable cover—a still on a fiery-orange background taken from the film *The Man Who Fell to Earth*—*Low* relaunches Bowie's position as a guru of avant-garde European rock. Not all critics of the period, however, will be able to perceive its revolutionary impact. Even less will RCA, which will slow down its promotion, considering it too uncommercial. But *Low* also marks a crucial stage in the English artist's personal rebirth. Through the assortment of mental pathologies—neurosis, agoraphobia, isolation, nihilism, apathy—explored in his lyrics, Bowie exorcises all the demons of the time, finding comfort in music as well as in the secluded dimension of his new life in Berlin. After years spent in the spotlight, he enjoys the anonymity that the city offers him. He stops dyeing his hair red, grows a moustache, and relaxes by painting, riding his bike, visiting art galleries, and going nightclubbing with the inseparable Iggy. Years later, recalling that period, he would declare, "I can't express the sense of freedom I felt!" And again: "Berlin was my clinic. It brought me back to the streets; not the streets where everyone is cold and there are drugs, but the ones where there are people who don't just think about how much they'll earn. Berliners are interested in art on the streets, not just in galleries."

David rents a seven-room apartment at 155 Hauptstrasse in the Schöneberg district. He experiences a phase of intense creative fervor, to the point of starting to shape the successor to *Low* just a few months after its

release, but not before having completed work on Iggy Pop's second solo LP, *Lust for Life*.

For the second chapter of the Berlin saga, which will also remain the only one entirely made in the German city, a stellar team is formed at Hansa Tonstudio: with Bowie (vocals, keyboards, guitars, saxophone, and koto) and Eno (synthesizers, keyboards, guitar treatments), there are Robert Fripp, guitarist and leader of King Crimson as well as author with Eno of two albums that can be defined as true "time machines," Carlos Alomar (guitar), Dennis Davis (percussion), and George Murray (bass), under the direction of the trusted Visconti. The sessions for *Heroes* take place at Hansa By the Wall Studio 2, a former ballroom in Weimar used by the Gestapo for recreational purposes in the 1930s and transformed into a recording studio. A legendary location, which Visconti remembers as follows: "It was a very large space. Just 400 meters from East Berlin, from the Wall. From my desk I could see three Soviet Red Guards looking at us through binoculars, with their rifles on their shoulders, the barbed wire, and I knew there were mines buried in the Wall. The atmosphere was exciting and frightening."

Left: The cover of Low, *and an image of Bowie at Heathrow Airport, before flying out to tour in the US and Canada, March 16, 1978*
Above: Bowie with Eno and Fripp in the studios in Berlin during the recording of "Heroes," (1977)

The recordings proceeded quickly, once again in the name of maximum creative freedom. Fripp, in fact, did everything in about six hours, as soon as he got off the plane from New York. "He arrived at the studio at 11 p.m., I hooked him up to the synthesizer for the effects, we played him everything we had done, and he started without even knowing the sequence of the chords," Visconti would recall. But it was the absolute monarch of King Crimson who created the guitar trademark that helped make *"Heroes"* (with the ironic quotation marks added to lighten the mood), if possible, even more dazzling than its predecessor, starting with the amazing distorted riffs of the song that gives it its title. "The sequence sounded grandiose and heroic, and I had that word, 'heroes,' in my mind," Eno would explain, while for biographer Chris O'Leary the inspiration was also the song "Hero" by the German band Neu!, all while in that period the Stranglers were releasing the punk anthem *No More Heroes*. The song's epic nature is indisputable, as is its compassionate spirit, which tries to cling to an optimistic future to exorcise a bitter present: "be heroes just for one day," even in everyday life. "It was an invitation to look reality in the face, drawing joy from the simple pleasure of being alive," its author will explain. The yearning for immortality ("for ever and ever") that tries to "steal the time" clashes with the inevitability of destiny, reaffirmed by the awareness that "nothing can keep us together."

According to the official version, "Heroes" was inspired by a pair of young lovers who met by the Wall

Around the narrative cue of the lyrics, for years Bowie circulated an "official version," according to which he was inspired by a young couple who used to meet under the Berlin Wall and whom he used to observe from a window of the Hansa Studios. Later, however, Visconti confessed that it was a fanciful interpretation of his real flirt with the chorister Antonia Maass, whom his friend had diplomatically "protected" so as not to ruin his marriage. Among the artistic sources of the song, however, there are the expressionist painting *Lovers Between Garden Walls* by Otto Mueller (1916), depicting a pair of lovers embracing between two looming walls, a symbol of the Great War, and the story *Una tomba per un delfino* by the Italian Alberto Denti di Pirajno, which tells the love story between an Italian soldier and a Somali girl during the Second World War.

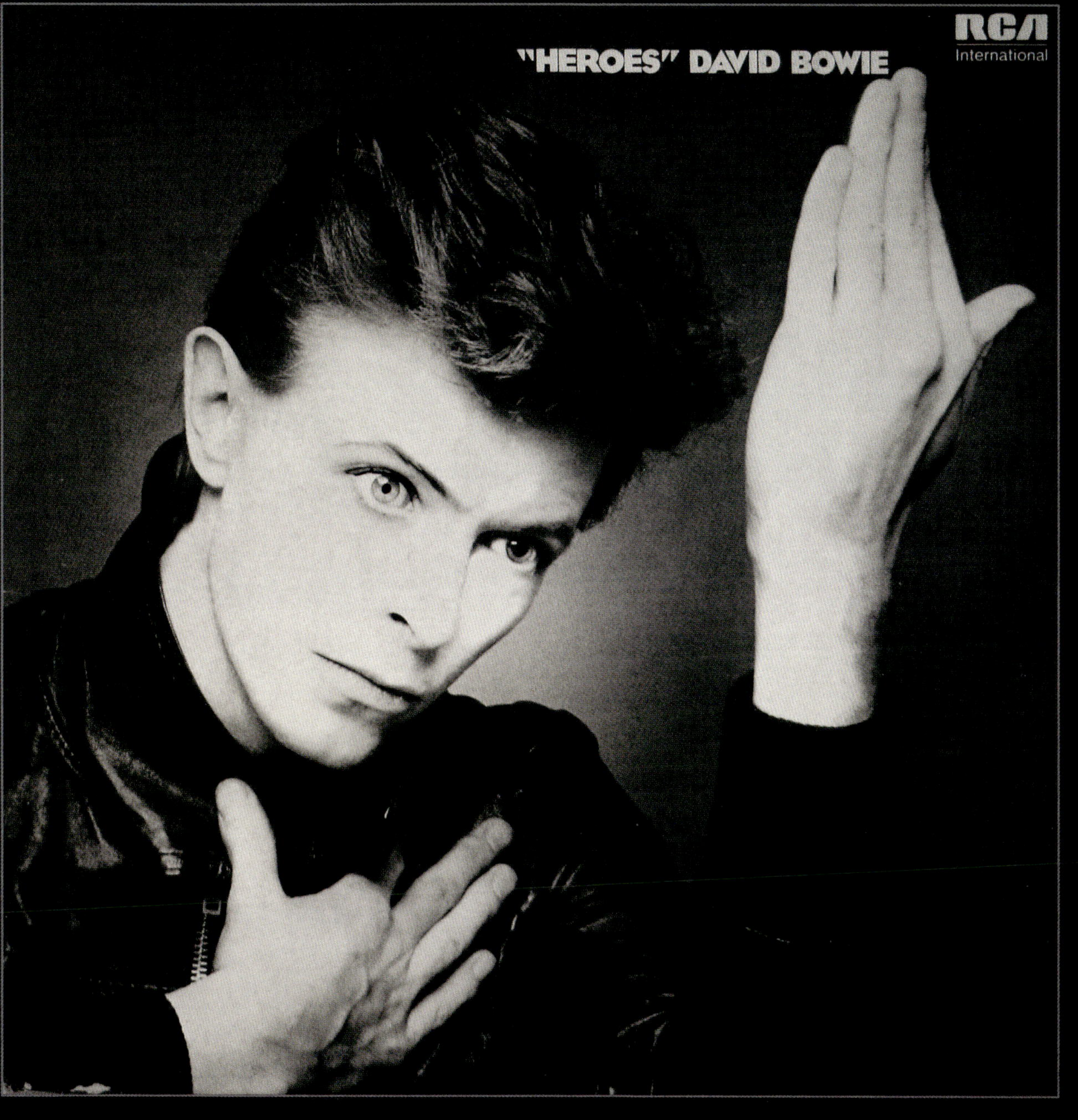

The cover of "Heroes" by Masayoshi Sukita, inspired by the works of German artist Erich Heckel, in particualr Roquairol*, which also inspired the cover for the album* The Idiot *by Iggy Pop. Featuring Bowie's contribution, the album was released the same year as "Heroes."*

With its trail of drones and feedback, Fripp's magical guitar line makes history, merging with the circular harmonies of Eno and his Ems synthesizer. *"Heroes"* is the paradigm of the perfect Bowie song, also embellished by a splendid vocal performance, which oscillates from a subdued emission to full-throat singing, reaching heights of heartbreaking intensity. Also ingenious is the method devised by Visconti to record the voice: a "multilatch" system, with three microphones positioned at different distances, which open in succession, creating a reverb effect.

Between plastic pop songs, dreams, and ambient fluctuations, *"Heroes"* lets some rays of light filter through, whereas *Low* was only black desolation. However, the avant-garde atmospheres and the bipartition of the track list remain, which latter places almost all the sung tracks on the first side and the more rarefied experiments on the second side.

In the opening "Beauty and the Beast," the glam essences of Roxy Music marry with a hard-core guitar riff and a beat rhythm pierced by Bowie's sly voice. "Joe the Lion" is a new guitar blast from Fripp, with David scripting the protagonist's delirium. Placed in the playlist after the title track, "Sons of the Silent Age" is the other emotional peak of the album: a ballad full of desperation, in which the breathtaking beginning, with the alienating sax by the Thin White Duke, gives way, almost like a siren, to a sumptuous chorus, in a sort of distorted R&B, while in the background a spectral choir rises. The lyrics are a decadent portrait of catatonic youth from the urban suburbs "standing on platforms with empty gazes, without books": "They make love only once / but they dream . . . / They don't walk, they slide / in and out of life / They never die, but one day they'll fall asleep."

The sonic schizophrenia of "Blackout," among unusual vocal harmonies, bursts of strident synths, and new guitar acrobatics, is already projected into new wave, while in the robotic V-2 Schneider (an ambiguous reference to the German bombs that were supposed to guarantee Hitler's victory, and at the same time a dedication to Kraftwerk's Florian Schneider), the Thin White Duke gives a dissonant sax performance on synthetic arrows and pressing drumming: It is the episode that acts as a bridge between the two sections of the album, ferrying the listener into the icy scenarios of the second part, where the atmospheres become more abstract, bordering on the ambient music and new age of many years later.

Eno's ghostly keyboards chisel the misty "Sense of Doubt"; the Japanese Zen watercolor of "Moss Garden" sees Bowie grappling with a duet between koto and synthesizer, while the expressionist fresco of "Neukölln"—dedicated to the high-density Turkish neighborhood of Berlin—is disfigured by the piercing high notes of a sax that sounds like an oriental instrument. The scenario changes for the finale: from the central European mists to the desert of "The Secret Life of Arabia," for a dance rock built on Middle Eastern scales. It's the ideal link with the subsequent *Lodger* (1979), in which the ethnic inputs will be explored in depth.

Blending Bowie's expressionist sensibility with Eno's oblique genius and Fripp's reckless guitar playing, *"Heroes"* marks a formal milestone in the hybridization process of rock and electronics. Berlin remains in the background, the ideal canvas of the Thin White Duke's healing psychodrama, but also a metaphor for his sense of anguish and alienation, well depicted in the paintings of expressionist painters, one of which—Erich Heckel's *Roquairol*—will also inspire the black-and- white cover image (curated by Japanese photographer Masayoshi Sukita).

RCA sensed the potential of the album this time, coining the effective slogan "There's Old Wave. There's New Wave. And there's David Bowie." *"Heroes"* will conquer both the critics—*Melody Maker* and *NME* will declare it album of the year—and the public, who will push it up to no. 3 in the UK (it will do less well in the US, where it will stop at no. 35).

With the *Low*-*"Heroes"* double album, Bowie coined a new sonic language, destined to influence an entire generation of bands—from Joy Division to Depeche Mode, from the Cure to Siouxsie and the Banshees, passing through Ultravox, Japan, and Simple Minds. Instead of sitting down to contemplate the flowering of that punk that he had unknowingly helped generate with Ziggy Stardust, the London dandy once again placed himself elsewhere, at the outpost of a new wave where part of the ex-punk scene would flow. "The whole punk movement was already over when I became aware of it," he would admit years later. "The few punk bands I saw in Berlin struck me above all for the fact that they were a sort of replica of the post-1969 Iggy; it seemed to me that they were all things that he had already done."

After the unsuccessful experiment of *David Live*, Bowie decides to capture his sonic breakthrough in a new live album. Only four years have passed, but between the glam pantomimes of the ginger-haired alien and the sound of *Stage* (1978), it seems like an eternity has passed. So, it was decided to feature the songs from the early period on side A, dedicating the rest of the double LP respectively to three songs from the American years (side B) and to a sort of "best of" of the Berlin works on the other two sides. And this time, the sound is much more convincing. Recorded during four dates of the Isolar II tour in Philadelphia, Providence, and Boston in 1978, *Stage* sounds in hi-fi almost as if it had been made in the studio. Even though the only overdub performed will be "Station to Station" (with intro and outro captured in Boston and the central part played in Providence): a hybrid version that will work so well that it will become the most beloved version, after having also been used in the cult concert scene in the film *Christiane F.—We Children from Bahnhof Zoo* (1981).

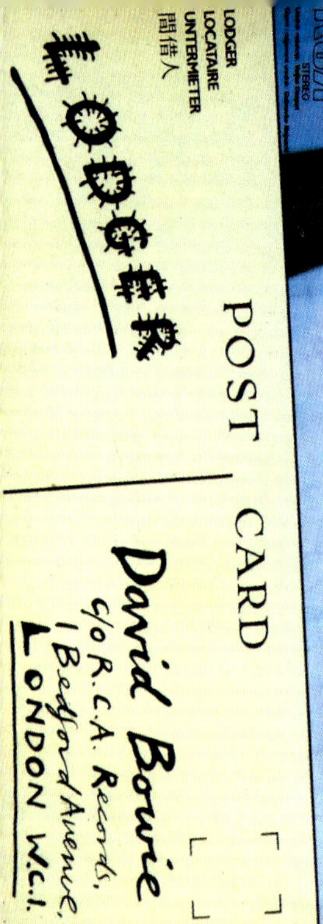

The cover of Lodger *(1979): a wide-shot image by Brian Duffy portraying Bowie with arms and legs spread apart on white tiles, with his nose and mouth pressed against a sheet of glass. Around him are scribbled versions of the album title in four different languages.*

From a lucky combination of the winning team of Berlin records and some of the new musicians hired for the Isolar II Tour, a new team was formed that began working on *Lodger*, the third chapter of the trilogy (although recorded in Montreux, Switzerland, and in New York). Visconti, Eno, Alomar, Murray, and Davis were joined by Sean Mayes (piano), Roger Powell (synth), Simon House (violin), and the acrobatic guitarist Adrian Belew, “stolen” from Frank Zappa’s group and also destined to join the court of King Crimson, from 1981.

Experimentation becomes even more acute, also anticipating the use of loops. While Eno increases the use of his Oblique Strategies, the musicians are asked to transform imperfections into arrangements. It is no coincidence that the working titles of the album were also *Planned Accidents and Despite Straight Lines*. “David often listened to the tapes and took the section with the most errors, which, repeated, became an integral part of the song,” Mayes revealed. The false starts of “African Night Flight” and “Repetition” become the gimmick to ignite new grooves while "Move On" was born as a sort of inverted version of the melody of "All the Young Dudes." In some cases, the musicians were even invited to exchange instruments, as in the spectacular power-trash-pop "Boys Keep Swinging," embellished by Bowie's histrionic singing and Belew's monstrous guitar solo, capable of mimicking even the most-extravagant noises. No less powerful is the other 45, "DJ," a perverse disco-funk crossover on dissonances of guitars and violins (recorded backward), which shows off another dazzling slogan-verse: "I am a DJ; I am what a play."

Although abandoning the ambient dilations in favor of a more classical but always incisive song form—well exemplified by the menacing "Look Back in Anger," *Lodger* presents itself as the logical culmination of that research into ethnic music, only sketched out in the previous chapters of the trilogy. Among the most successful experiments in this sense, the trip with (red) sails spread out of "Red Sails," whose incessant motorik beat à la Neu! mixes with Middle Eastern spices, but also the Arabian reggae hybrid of Yassassin and the Afro-funk tribal march of "African Night Flight." The result of this experience will be included in Eno's baggage and, together with Fela Kuti's records, will also go on to compose the Afro-rock canvas of Talking Heads' "Remain in Light."

World music is just around the corner: It will be up to Peter Gabriel to be its standard-bearer in the '80s, leading a group of musicians who, from David Byrne to Japan, from Paul Simon to Kate Bush, will cross new frontiers. The intuition is among the most farsighted of Bowie's career, but he will give up on boasting about it, acknowledging Eno as the father of the turning point: "I never completed what would have been called world beat," he will declare. "Brian did it. I think some songs we wrote together, like 'African Night Flight,' gave him the push to continue with things like *My Life in the Bush of Ghosts* [the 1981 album with Byrne]. He found the idea of combining ethnic music with a Western rhythm stimulating."

The lyrics become even more cryptic, revealing unusual reflections on social and political issues, as in the case of "Repetition," on the theme of domestic violence, and "Fantastic Voyage," which behind the soft rhythms and courageous vocal lines hides an exhortation to stop the arms race ("It's a moving world, but that's no reason / to shoot some of those missiles"). The cover is also unusual: a wide-angle photo by Brian Duffy portraying Bowie with his arms and legs open in the middle of white tiles, with his nose and mouth pressed against a pane of glass, among scribbled inscriptions with the title of the album in four languages, to reiterate the idea of the journey, already extolled in the dreamlike ode of "Move On" ("Somethimes I feel / The need to move on / So I pack a bag / And move on"). A "Fantastic Voyage" that ends with "Red Money," twin sister of "Sister Midnight," already included in *The Idiot* by Iggy Pop, which the English friend has fun reinterpreting in his own way.

The critics, once again, are taken aback and divided, while the public drags the album to fourth place in the British charts and to no. 20 in the US. Although it marks the incursion into new sonic frontiers, the bold—and underrated—experience of *Lodger* is the perfect conclusion to the Berlin trilogy. Three albums animated by an extraordinary innovative charge that will germinate in countless styles and bands up to the present day. Their charm will not escape even a classically trained composer like the master of minimalism, Philip Glass, who will call them "works of genius" and will translate some symphonic pieces into a new trilogy.

In the meantime, Bowie records a new version of *Peter and the Wolf* with the Philadelphia Orchestra, in the role of narrator. He returned to the set for David Hemmings's *Gigolo*. And he appeared in top form on TV at *Saturday Night Live*, where he performed in costumes inspired by Dada theater. The two years of German exile transformed him into a more complete and mature artist. "I felt more serene and productive," he would later say. "I spent my days reading, writing, and painting." But "if something works, throw it away" was the refrain of his life. So it was time for another change, to return to the United States. The definitive farewell to Berlin would be sanctioned a year later, with a new album and a new turning point.

The two years of German exile transformed Bowie: "Berlin was my clinic. I felt more serene and productive."

David Bowie in a scene from the film Gigolo*, during filming in West Berlin, February 6, 1978*

4

THE GLOBAL SUPERSTAR OF THE '80S

DANCING ON THE EDGE **OF MAINSTREAM** IN THE TECHNICOLOR DECADE

Sound and images: two inseparable components in the art of David Bowie. Of all the members of the rock aristocracy, the Thin White Duke was the most aware of the value of images and the most skilled at exploiting them. He had developed a pioneering aptitude for video clips in the '70s, which in the following decade—the MTV era—he would have fully mastered, placing himself at the forefront (also) of the glittering season of video music. Among the first testimonies of this vocation, in addition to the evocative clip of "Life on Mars?," we should remember the triptych of singles from *Lodger:* starting with "DJ," one of the first songs with a visual commentary elaborated thanks to director David Mallet, who captures Bowie in the role of the neurasthenic protagonist of the song as he destroys his equipment and then strolls around London. Then, "Boys Keep Swinging," in which the English dandy sings surrounded by a trio of girls who are none other than three images of Bowie in drag, before taking off his wig and destroying his makeup by running his hand over his face, just as he had seen done in transvestite shows in Berlin. Finally, the disturbing Dorian Grayesque prophecy of "Look Back in Anger," in which a painter sees his face deteriorate while caressing the perfect face of a painted angel.

Always aware of the importance of image, Bowie also put himself at the forefront of the 80s music video season

The relationship with Mallet will mark the entire pioneering phase of Bowie's video clips, up to the famous promos for the album *Let's Dance* and the video concert *Serious Moonlight.*

But the decisive moment comes with the new single that Bowie creates at the dawn of the '80s. The concept of the video clip as we conceive it today, in fact, was born with the four minutes of film shot by Mallet in 1980 for "Ashes to Ashes." As Lorenzo Salzano points out on *OndaRock*, "The editing of surreal images with a disturbing subtext, the experimentation with optical effects such as chromakey, the very fact that the film is based on a storyboard designed by the singer with the director, make *Ashes to Ashes* the first music video capable of going beyond the simple task of promoting a song, transforming itself into a new medium." According to David Buckley, it will also be the most expensive video shot at the time (around £250,000). For the occasion, Bowie unleashes a new character: a hallucinated Pierrot, created by costume designer Natasha Korniloff, already in Lindsay Kemp's entourage. He is the protagonist of the video's procession, set on a beach near Hastings, England. Almost a funeral procession, led by the clown, with a priest, two nuns, and a girl dressed up for the occasion, followed by a menacing excavator. In a dreamlike sequence, the images alternate with an astronaut hanging from a monstrous *Alien*-style machine, a prisoner in an exploding kitchen, then in a room with padded walls, before cutting back to the beach, where the Pierrot, already warned by an old woman (David's mother?), sinks into the sea, and a funeral pyre burns images and outlines. Ashes to ashes.

In *Ashes To Ashes*, Major Tom returns, transformed into a junkie, lost in never-ending depression.

Between the catchy refrain of Chuck Hammer's guitar synth, off-beat rhythms, and synthetic strings, counterpointed by Bowie's powerful funky bass and layered vocals, "Ashes to Ashes" would be a masterpiece even on a purely musical level. But what will also enchant the audience, who will drag it to the top of the UK Chart, will be its video, a visionary expression of complex intertextual references: starting with the return of Major Tom from "Space Oddity" transformed into a drug addict lost in an endless depression. It is yet another alter ego on which Bowie pours all his demons, from drug addiction to the excesses of his rock star career ("I never did good things / I never did bad things / I never did anything out of the blue").

Placing himself at the forefront of the new music video season, the Bowie of "Ashes to Ashes" also becomes a pioneer of a new subculture that is taking root in Great Britain in those days. A sort of new glamorous era that unites degenerate children of punk, irremediably corrupted by a decadent and narcissistic taste. It is the new romantic season, which will borrow the nonconformist ideology of glam rock in a new intoxication of gaudy looks and cultural provocations. Here then are pirates with stylized makeup, effeminate chic, kids dressed up in geometric clothes, and neo-aristocrats with coiffed hair. Leading them was Welshman Steve Strange, a stirrer of London nightlife with his Blitz Club and member of Visage, one of the key groups of the new scene, along with

Ultravox, Spandau Ballet, Duran Duran, Culture Club, Adam & the Ants, and Human League & Co. For many of them, Bowie's appearance on *Top of the Pops* with Starman in 1972 represented a sort of initiation rite. And it was precisely the Thin White Duke's Berlin songs—in addition to classics by Moroder, Kraftwerk, and Roxy Music—that took center stage at the Blitz console, in the hands of DJ Rusty Egan.

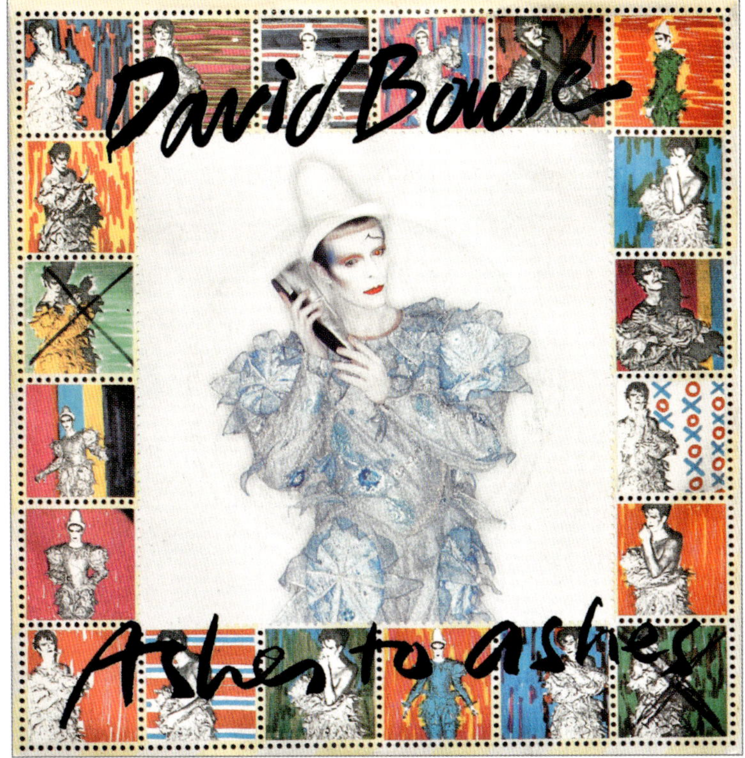

Intrigued, Bowie decides to go down the steps of the Covent Garden basement to recruit the extras for the "Ashes to Ashes" video among the devotees who threw wild parties in his honor. A messianic event, that of July 1, 1980, which the protagonists will recount with intact emotion in the definitive documentary of that season, *Blitzed!* (2020). The four lucky ones who will stand out in eccentric clothes among the sunbursts of the famous short sound film will be Strange himself, the designer Judith Frankland, the stylist Darla-Jane Gilroy, and the future model Elise Brazier. In one swoop, with the "Ashes to Ashes" video, Bowie put himself at the head of the dawning music-video era and a new declination of the new wave in a new romantic key. Not all of the '80s will continue for him in such an inspired way, but the beginning is truly explosive. And a new album is on the way, *Scary Monsters*, which the most-diehard fans and critics will even identify as the last essential chapter of his career.

Bowie shows up free from the toxic influences of the '70s and fresh from a divorce. On February 8, 1980, the end of his marriage to Angela Barnett will be sealed, who will entrust him with their son, Zowie, the future Duncan Jones. At the Power Station Studios in New York, waiting for him is the faithful Visconti and the rhythm section Alomar/Davis/Murray, while Andy Clark and Roy Bittan take turns on the keyboards. Special guest, once again his crimson majesty Robert Fripp, who will play most of the guitar solos (with some overdubs by the newcomer Chuck Hammer) and Pete Townshend of the Who, who takes up the guitar on "Because You're Young." The work will be completed at the Good Earth in London, in April.

The monsters on *Scary Monsters (and Super Creeps)* are above all the inner demons that Bowie decides to deal with, in a sort of controlled exorcism: "It was a kind of purge," he said: "I was the one who uprooted from inside the feelings that I felt uncomfortable with." The result is an album that is fully immersed in that new-wave era of which Bowie is a pioneer and that he now celebrates, in the tribute to Tom Verlaine's *Television* (the cover of "Kingdom Come"), but at the same time gives a warning, ironically addressing those who would like to put him on a pedestal in "Teenage Wildlife": "You're a big shot with a broken nose / One of the new wave kids / The same old thing dressed up in a new guise / Coming on the scene, oh-ooh / Ugly like a teenage billionaire / Pretending it's a magical world." "I imagine it's aimed at a phantom teenage brother, if I had one," he explains, "trying to approach a young mind, which is not prepared for hypocrisy. It's an invitation to accept change, rather than become reactionary."

Bowie pays tribute to the new wave he pioneered and at the same time warns those who would put him on a pedestal

Page 119: Bowie as Pierrot drawn by Natasha Korniloff for the video of "Ashes to Ashes," for the cover of the album (page 121), and for the cover of Scary Monsters (and Super Creeps), *the 1980 album (left)*
Right: The cover of the single "Fashion," released in 1980

The other single, "Fashion," also stands out, accompanied by a new video by Mallet in which Bowie performs in front of a robotic audience, who react mechanically to his every move. A witty parody of consumer society, built on funk-reggae rhythms, with a bass line and a melody along the lines of "Golden Years." While Fripp asserts himself with his high-pitched and dissonant guitar, Bowie has the opportunity to stage another grotesque pantomime with his singing, pillorying the world of fashion with contemptuous lines such as "Fashion! Turn to the left / Fashion! Turn to the right," and "Listen to me, don't listen to me." "I think fashion is a funny thing," he will comment. "It's probably because of its nonsense nature that it seems that way to me. We shouldn't follow it."

Fripp's trademark guitar playing is also evident in the pressing title track, where Bowie narrates the story of a woman falling into madness in a wall of synthesized percussion, and in the burning overture "It's No Game (Part 1)," in which actress Michi Hirota's declamations in Japanese alternate with the broken, ferocious singing of the Thin White Duke, who will reveal that he used that shrill, almost feminine tone "to break a particular type of sexist attitude" about Japanese girls and women in general. The second part, "It's No Game (Part 2)," placed at the end of the set list, sounds much more relaxed, as if the anger that permeates the grooves of the album—from the outburst on divorce in "Up the Hills Backwards" to the antitotalitarian invective in "Scream Like a Baby"—had now faded.

THE
LEPHANT MA

As the perfect link between Bowie's avant-garde phase and his subsequent pop evolution, with his new alter ego Pierrot appearing on Edward Bell's cover illustration, *Scary Monsters* also convinced RCA, who coined the new slogan "Often Copied, Never Equaled," referring to the new-wave artists whom Bowie had inspired. And the fruits were to be seen, with the album once again reaching the top of the UK Chart, six years after *Diamond Dogs*, plus a remarkable no. 12 in the USA, the best result since *Low*.

Scary Monsters, however, will not have any live promotion, because Bowie in the meantime had already been engaged in other projects: for example, the play *The Elephant Man*, by the American playwright Bernard Pomerance, inspired by the film of the same title by David Lynch, in which he plays the protagonist Joseph Merrick. In this period, however, an unexpected collaboration also arrives, which will yield an everlasting hit.

"Under Pressure" was born out of a session between two strong personalities and became the perfect union of two different approaches.

In July 1981, Bowie is at the Mountain Studios in Montreux with Giorgio Moroder to record the single "Cat People." In the adjacent studio, Freddie Mercury's Queen are recording their new LP, *Hot Space*. It is the opportunity for two of the greatest front men in the history of rock to meet, united by their theatrical attitude and sexually ambiguous image, as well as their common militancy in the glam movement. "Under Pressure" was born spontaneously, during a joint session, and is the fruit of two charismatic personalities. "It wasn't easy to work together: David and Freddie clashed. But that's also why the song became fantastic," Queen guitarist Brian May will reveal. The song is a sort of pop Frankenstein of the authors' different approaches: with the scat intro and the stadium chorus ("Give love another chance") typical of Queen, the break on the words "insanity laughs" unmistakably Bowian, as well as the final verse ("This is our last dance"), for a sort of "pendulum that oscillates between the refined art rock of Bowie and the charged glam of Queen."

David Bowie onstage at the Booth Theatre on Broadway, New York, September 18, 1980, during the performance of The Elephant Man

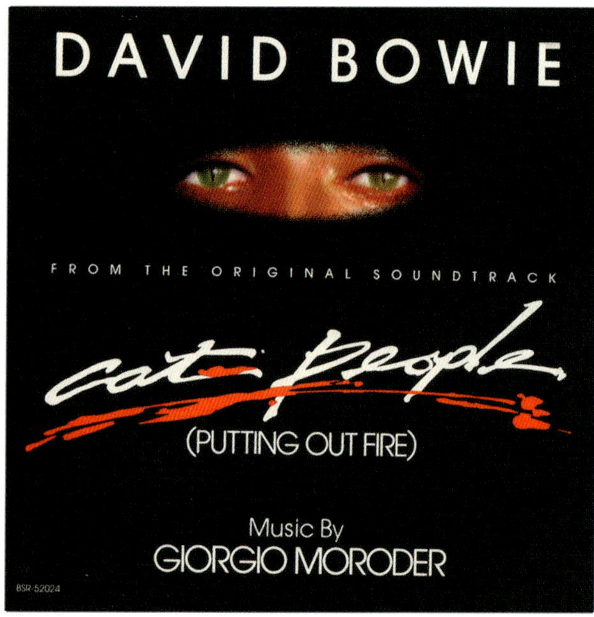

Making it a success (no. 1 in the UK) will also be the unmistakable bass line by John Deacon of Queen. The latter will regularly include "Under Pressure" in the set lists of their shows, while Bowie will perform it live for the first time in the duet with Annie Lennox at the Freddie Mercury Tribute Concert in 1992, the event at Wembley in memory of the singer, who had died a year earlier from bronchopneumonia aggravated by AIDS-related complications.

The other big hit of the period is the aforementioned "Cat People (Putting Out Fire)," produced with Moroder, the man who had invented Donna Summer's sparkling disco music with "I Feel Love" and who had made Eno exclaim, "I've heard the sound of the future." The song was intended to complete the soundtrack of the homonymous film *Cat People* by Paul Schrader. The result is another dazzling example of Bowie crooning, with a cavernous baritone counterbalanced by a chorus of female voices, for a number with dark undertones, in tune with the dark atmosphere of the film. The glossy version included a year later on *Let's Dance* was less incisive. Before the new album, there will be time for another experiment: David Bowie in Bertolt Brecht's *Baal*, the EP with the five songs that Bowie performed in the teledrama *Baal*, an adaptation of Brecht's play of the same name, directed by Alan Clarke.

Above: The cover of the 45 LP "Cat People (Putting Out Fire)," created with Giorgio Moroder in 1982
Right: Bowie with Otis Blackwell and Nile Rodgers of Chic at the Urban Contemporary Awards at the Savoy in New York, January 21, 1983

The three-year break between *Scary Monsters* and *Let's Dance* is not accidental. Bowie decides to free himself from RCA and signs with EMI. In addition, he waits for the fateful expiration of the agreement with Defries (September 30, 1982), which allows him to obtain all the rights. In the meantime, he returns to the set for the film *Merry Christmas Mr. Lawrence* by Nagisa Oshima, spending several months in the South Pacific. During this period, he listens to some R&B compilations that reawaken his passion for Black music. The seeds of yet another turning point are planted, under the aegis of a new producer, with all due respect to his friend Tony Visconti, who does not take it well. The new producer was another dance guru, Nile Rodgers, who had added new hits to the console to the evergreens of his Chic (*Le Freak*, *Good Times*), at the court of Sister Sledge (*We Are Family*) and Diana Ross (*Upside Down*).

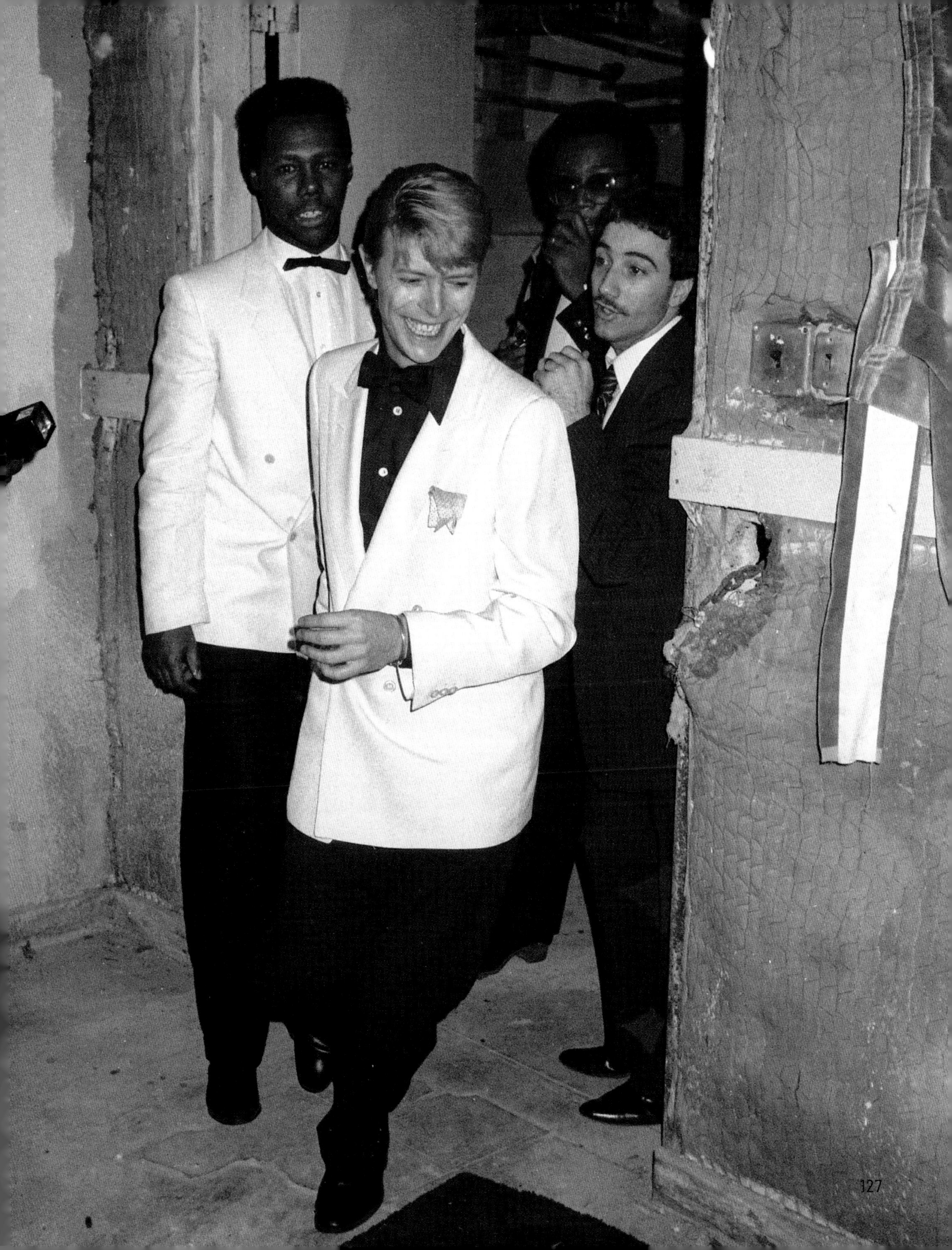

Bowie met Rodgers in New York and gave him a precise instruction: "I want you to make hits." The producer took him at his word. Thus was born *Let's Dance*, the album that would transform the ex-glam alien into a global star, storming to the top of the charts on both sides of the Atlantic.

The lineup for the *Let's Dance* sessions in Montreux, Switzerland, was also renewed. Bowie hired Texan guitarist Stevie Ray Vaughan and entrusted Rodgers with the choice of the other musicians—namely, Tony Thompson and Bernard Ed-wards, drummer and bassist of Chic; Rob Sabino (keyboards); and Sammy Figueroa (percussion); plus the brothers Frank and George Simms on backing vocals, drummer Omar Hakim (formerly of Weather Report), Puerto Rican bassist Carmine Rojas, and a horn section from the Asbury Jukes.

Above: Bowie as a boxer for the cover of the album Let's Dance *(1983)*
Right: The covers of the two 45 LP: "China Girl" (with New Zealand model Geeling Ng, present in the music video as well) and "Modern Love"

The sudden shift toward a more danceable sound immediately yields a hit: the persuasive title track, with a dance groove à la Chic, onto which Vaughan's guitar solo is grafted with controlled ferocity. Even if behind the dance in the moonlight ("under the moonlight, this serious moonlight"), there is a sense of unknown about the future: "Let's dance for fear your grace should fall / . . . for fear this night is all"—"Let's dance for fear your grace should fall / . . . for fear this night is all"—"Let's dance for fear / You could lose your grace / Let's dance for fear tonight." Also making an impact on the charts will be the other 45 rpm, "China Girl," a glossy cover of the rock song by Iggy Pop (from *The Idiot*), thanks to Bowie's sensual singing, the

sticky oriental guitar riff created by Rodgers, and a video in which a naked Thin White Duke is portrayed together with the New Zealand model (of Asian origins) Geeling Ng on an exotic Australian beach. "It's a vignette depicting my lifelong infatuation with all things Asian," Bowie explained. The alleged parody of the geisha stereotype would give rise to criticism, and the inevitable censorship would fall on the hottest images. In reality, with its painful lyrics, "China Girl" aligns itself with the themes of cultural identity and hopeless love that dominate the album.

Completing the trio of 45 rpm hits is the "dive bar rock" (Rodgers's words) of "Modern Love," with its pounding piano, wall of percussion, and ringing sax inserts supporting the call-and-response vocals, inspired by his idol Little Richard, and a reflection on the eternal conflict between God and man. If the new, smooth version of "Cat People" doesn't offer any particular interest compared to the original, the successful cover of Metro's "Criminal World" wraps a poignant melody in refined arrangements, while the bizarre "Ricochet" is perhaps the only foray into experimental territory, with its obsessive R&B-and-swing background and Bowie's desolate singing, which instead seems to lose the thread in other episodes ("Without You," "Shake It").

1 9 8 3

It is an ambiguous relationship, the one that binds the English artist to his six-million-copy bestseller, which for the first time will attract the accusation of having given in to commercial logic. After having justified the choice of not playing any instruments in the eight songs on the set list by claiming that it was a "singer's record," he will come to distance himself more openly. "I think *Let's Dance* was more of a Nile album than mine." And again: "It was Nile's vision of what my music should be; I just provided the songs." Then he will admit: "It put me in the position of telling my artistic integrity to go fuck itself. It was conceived as a separate project, and I had every intention of continuing in my usual style. But the success of that record forced me to continue flirting with the beast. It was my decision, but I felt, after a few years, that I was artistically blocked."

After *Let's Dance*, Bowie feels stuck: the magnificence of the *Serious Moonlight Tour* will mask his crisis

The creative crisis was brilliantly masked by the sumptuous Serious Moonlight Tour, touring fifteen countries, with ninety-six shows and over 2.6 million tickets sold. A celebration of the myth of Bowie, who showed off his new peroxide rocker look already shown on the cover (in the guise of a boxer) and in the videos of *Let's Dance*. A new creature in a suit and tie, surrounded by a formidable ensemble of musicians and breathtaking choreography, for pharaonic sets that reviewed his hits in rock, pop, and funk.

David Bowie performs onstage in "Cracked Actor," during the European leg of the Serious Moonlight Tour, 1983.

But the success of the album and the tour turned out to be a boomerang for an artist who had always been incapable of resting on his laurels. "I looked at the sea of people who came to the concerts, and asked myself: How many Velvet Underground records do they have at home? I quickly felt alienated from my audience. And it was depressing, because I didn't know what they wanted." It is yet another Bowie paradox: Just after having achieved the worldwide success he had been aiming for since the days of Ziggy Stardust, he found himself in a dead end that would lead him to reach the lowest point of his career in the following years.

Left: Bowie plays the saxophone during the Serious Moonlight Tour in 1983.
Above: Bowie performs at the Feijenoord "de Kuip" Stadium in Rotterdam, June 25, 1983, as part of the Serious Moonlight Tour.

While the release of the concert film *Ziggy Stardust and the Spiders from Mars*, shot on 16 mm by DA Pennebaker, reawakens nostalgia for the glam alien, consigned to history in that very show on July 3, 1973, at London's Hammersmith Odeon, Bowie is ready to turn the page. He also bids farewell to Rodgers and decides to rely on a new producer, Derek Bramble, to prove that his music can sustain itself without the help of a famous "hitmaker." But he lacks songs. So much so that in the end, *Tonight* will contain only a couple of his unreleased songs ("Blue Jean" and "Loving the Alien"), as well as two pieces written with Iggy Pop ("Tumble and Twirl" and "Dancing with the Big Boys") and five covers, including songs by Iguana and other authors.

Tonight's lack of ideas is evident right from the faded single-appetizer "Blue Jean," played on horns and old-fashioned rock 'n' roll riffs, with its accompanying video by Julian Temple (short version for MTV and twenty-one-minute short "Jazzin' for Blue Jeans"), in which Bowie doubles up playing the clumsy Vic and the heavily made-up rock star Screaming Lord Byron. And if the reggae of the title track (a remake of a track from Pop's *Lust for Life*) essentially serves as a backdrop to the stellar duet with Tina Turner, the up-tempo funk of the exotic "Tumble and Twirl" runs on empty, as does the overloaded cover of the Beach Boys' "God Only Knows."

In a flat set list, the opening is an exception, entrusted to a splendid new composition: "Loving the Alien" shines with its poignant melodic opening, declaimed at the top of Bowie's voice, in the majestic string arrangement by Arif Mardin. Despite the title, it is not a return to the beloved science-fiction scenarios, but rather a harsh invective against organized religions, with references to the horrors of the Crusades and disinformation as an instrument of power.

But that feat won't be enough to redeem *Tonight*. "It's a reject, and Bowie knows it," *Rolling Stone* will declare. Accustomed to being pampered by critics—or at least to divide them into opposing factions—Bowie has to deal with a general cold shower, which will not be mitigated by the new commercial success (no. 1 in the UK). He is aware that he has no longer been able to stay at the forefront, not even of that chart pop that in those years in the UK was living off new stars such as Marc Almond, Culture Club, Bronski Beat, and Frankie Goes to Hollywood—not to mention rock acts such as the Police, Dire Straits, Smiths, and the Cure—while on the other side of the ocean, phenomena such as Michael Jackson, Prince, and Madonna were raging.

By the mid-eighties, Bowie seems to have lost his way: he would have to wait until the new decade to make albums that lived up to his standards again. Yet, his creativity didn't wane. Two excellent singles released in 1985 bear witness to this. The first, "This Is Not America," was the result of a collaboration with the jazz giant the Pat Metheny Group, for the soundtrack of John Schlesinger's film *The Falcon and the Snowman.* An example of refined crooning, wrapped in elegant jazz-fusion textures, with Metheny grappling with the rhythm guitar, for a new message to the invasive culture of American capitalism. Another feat of 1985, "Absolute Beginners," was also destined for a soundtrack, the theme for Julian Temple's film of the same title, set in London in the late 1950s, in which Bowie starred alongside Sade and Patsy Kensit. Performed with a full throat, between a nostalgic melody and a lively doo-wop cadence, the song is embellished by Kevin Armstrong's guitar inserts, Rick Wakeman's (Yes) hammering piano, and a triumphant sax sound, which Bowie had spent a lot of time searching for in that period. It will climb to no. 2 in the UK Chart.

Less significant will be the contributions made a year later to the soundtrack of the film *Labyrinth* (with the exception of the poignant "When the Wind Blows"); on the other hand, Bowie will put his unmistakable mark on Iggy Pop's new album, *Blah-Blah-Blah*, collaborating on the writing of some songs and producing the album with David Richards. Thus a pearl like "Shades," marked by the dark song of the Iguana but Bowian to the core, will become the most precious outtake of the unfortunate tandem "Tonight"–"Never Let Me Down." Not by chance, Pop himself will almost disown the album, defining it as "a Bowie album in everything but name."

Left: The cover of the album Tonight *(1984) by Mick Haggerty, the designer behind the artwork in* Let's Dance*: Bowie is painted in blue against a backdrop of oil painting and flowers.*

In the meantime, Bowie was one of the main protagonists of the colossal Live Aid, the musical event organized by Bob Geldof and Midge Ure with the aim of raising funds for famine relief in Ethiopia. On July 13, 1985, at Wembley (London) and at the John Fitzgerald Kennedy Stadium in Philadelphia, many of the musical stars of the time took to the field. Initially, an intercontinental duet between Mick Jagger (in the USA) and David Bowie (in London) was also planned. However, synchronization problems prevented the transatlantic sleight of hand, so the two quickly created a video for the song they wanted to sing: a cover of "Dancing in the Street," a classic performed in 1964 by Martha and the Vandellas. Filmed by Mallet in one night in the London docklands, the film portrays the two rock aces busy making fun of each other. That would be enough for a new number-one hit. Onstage at Wembley, with Thomas Dolby on keyboards, Bowie will instead offer a varied set with "TVC 15," "Modern Love," "Rebel Rebel," and "Heroes," dedicating the latter to his young son, as well as "to children all over the world."

But if his popularity is skyrocketing, his inspiration is languishing. The last solo LP of the '80s, *Never Let Me Down* (1987), is commonly considered the lowest point of Bowie's career. Starting from its author himself: "It was my nadir, a bitter disappointment," he will admit. Recorded at Mountain Studios in Montreux with a mix of old and new musicians (Rojas, Alomar, and "the Borneo Horns" from *Tonight* are joined by guitarist Peter Frampton and multi-instrumentalist Erdal Kızılçay) and

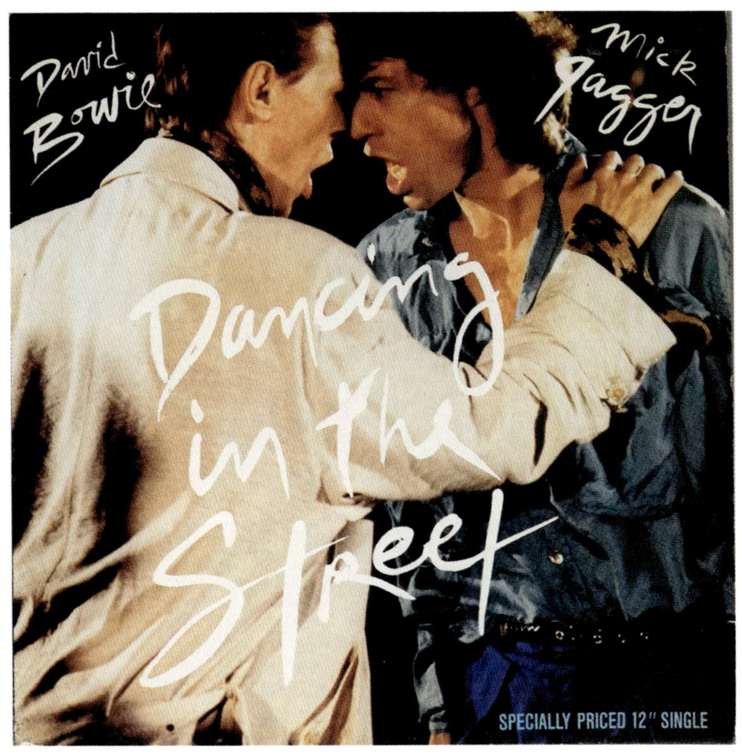

1985

Left: David Bowie onstage at Wembley Stadium, July 13, 1985, for Live Aid, organized by Bob Geldof and Midge Ure to raise money for famine-stricken Ethiopia
Second left: The cover of the single "Dancing in the Street," *by David Bowie and Mick Jagger*

produced by Bowie himself with Richards, it is a weak and confused work. In its intentions, it wants to be "a return to guitar rock," "an evolution starting from *Scary Monsters*" rather than from its two pop predecessors. In reality, it continues to wink at the charts, but without a refrain to match. Thus the set list founders, starting from the fake-aggressive and overproduced single "Day-In Day-Out," between emphatic percussions, redundant trumpets, and a dull guitar solo. And if side A is still keeping afloat with the strident chant of "Time Will Crawl" (inspired by the Chernobyl nuclear tragedy of 1986), the heartfelt Lennon-style ballad of the title track, dedicated to the inseparable Coco Schwab, and the psychedelic "Zeroes" (a mix of the Beatles' "Eight Days a Week," Traffic's hit "Paper Moon," and Prince's single "Little Red Corvette"), side B, after the encouraging guitar riff of the nursery rhyme "Glass Spider," slips into a downward spiral, drowning in flaccid pop-rock numbers like "Shining Star (Makin' My Love)," "New York's in Love," "'87 & Cry," and "Too Dizzy." A misstep that also nullifies Bowie's reinvigorated vocals, which have returned to soaring to higher tones, sometimes even into falsetto.

In the following years, the English artist would come to deny his 1984–1987 period altogether. "I wasn't interested in what I was doing, and I let everyone tell me what to do," he would say in 1993. "I let them arrange my songs, let the stylists propose what they thought were magnificent fashionable clothes. I didn't want to be disturbed. A wave of total numbness had hit me."

But another unscrupulous move comes to mask the crisis. Now cleansed of the excesses of the previous decade, a platinum-plated global star venerated by several generations of fans, Bowie embarks on a new, huge tour, which this time will earn him more than one criticism, both for the set lists—unbalanced in favor of the latest, disappointing LP—and for the excessive choreography. It is the infamous Glass Spider Tour, which gathers almost three million people in stadiums in fifteen countries for eighty-six concerts, with kitsch blockbuster sets, centered on a giant luminescent spider. A sort of 1980s *Rocky Horror Show*, in which the camp aesthetics and grotesque theatricality of the old Diamond Dogs Tour are transformed into an exaggerated circus setting, set up by set designer Mark Ravitz. Between bouffant hairdos and unlikely looks, the forty-year-old White Duke dances, runs, and jumps on stage, putting on a show of undoubted visual impact, surrounded by a dazzling band (Carlos Alomar, Peter Frampton, and Charlie Sexton on guitar; Carmine Rojas on bass; Alan Childs on drums; Erdal Kızılçay and Richard Cottle on keyboards) and five dancers, including Melissa Hurley, his partner at the time. The Glass Spider Tour will also mark Bowie's live return to Italy, eighteen years after his first historic incursion in 1969 in Monsummano Terme (Pistoia).

Above: The Glass Spider Tour at Festivalground in Werchter, Belgium, June 2, 1987
Right: A winged David Bowie towering onstage at the Glass Spider Tour (1987)

1 9 8 7

Left and above: Bowie dances onstage and hovers aboveground, while sitting on a throne supported by ropes, during the Belgian leg of the Glass Spider Tour in Werchter, June 2, 1987.

SEX LIES RELIGION

Having worn off the Glass Spider Tour hangover, Bowie was more aware than ever of the impasse he was trapped in: "Intoxicated by success, I had lost my natural enthusiasm for things. I felt like an empty vessel, and I feared I would end up like everyone else, doing these stupid fucking shows, singing 'Rebel Rebel' until I dropped dead." A spark was needed to rekindle his lost creativity. It would come in the form of a thirty-one-year-old American guitarist whom he met at the end of the tour. A graduate of the Berklee College of Music, Reeves Gabrels was an experimenter devoted to thunderous Fripp-inspired hard core. He told Bowie, "The only obstacle between doing what you want to do and what you think you should do is you." That was be enough to convince him. The London artist, determined to return to the roots of unfiltered rock 'n' roll, saw in him the man of providence. And he matures one of the most radical and controversial choices of his career: to become the front man of a hard-rock band. Thus Tin Machine was born, as a sort of return to lost integrity, a purifying catharsis of the hedonism and disengagement that followed the exploit of *Let's Dance*. The man who had become one of the greatest stars of world rock simply transforms himself into a member of a band, playing in small clubs, as if he wanted to seek a new anonymity after the one that had made him come back to life in Berlin.

The two LPs under the name Tin Machine, however, will not remain engraved in the history of rock. More effective, perhaps, is the first *Tin Machine* (1989), recorded by the duo Gabrels-Bowie with the Sales brothers (Tony on bass and Hunt on drums) and guitarist Armstrong between Montreux and Nassau (Bahamas). Poised between blues and hard rock, the album displays a raw and noisy sound, which has its peaks in the vibrant invective of "I Can't Read," with Gabrels's sharp guitar line and Bowie's painful interpretation, in the pressing "Crack City," and in the blues-rock of "Prisoner of Love," which culminates in a quote from Ginsberg's famous *Howl*. After a fleeting leap to third place in the UK charts, *Tin Machine* will disappear from the radar, sowing distrust even among critics—who, however, in some cases, will recognize the courage of such radical change. More merciless will be the reactions to the subsequent *Tin Machine II* (1991), where only a few episodes ("Baby Universal," "Goodbye Mr. Ed") attempt to offer a more refined structure to a sound now drowned in a chaotic din, and to the botched live LP *Tin Machine Live: Oy Vey, Baby* of 1992. Yet, it will be precisely the jolt of Tin Machine that will reactivate Bowie's energy, ferrying him into the experiments of the following decade.

The experience with Tin Machine did not leave any memorable records, but it reactivated Bowie's energy, who was ready to return to his best shape.

A promotional image of Tin Machine in 1991. From the left: Tony Sales, Hunt Sales, David Bowie, and Reeves Gabrels.

5

THE SOUND INVESTIGATIONS OF A RECKLESS OUTSIDER

THE HI-TECH '90S OF A **POSTINDUSTRIAL HERO** HUNGRY FOR EXPERIMENTATION

In the midst of the daring adventure of Tin Machine, Bowie had tried to reconcile himself with his fans—who were left shocked and incredulous—by reproposing his most beloved solo repertoire in a new tour, Sound+Vision, which had kept him busy for most of 1990, landing in 27 countries with 108 concerts. Onstage, once again flanked by Belew, the Thin White Duke was resurrected in his fullness as a rock star, using for the first time a giant screen to project videos, with strong nostalgic effects: another formidable show, halfway between the jukebox of the Roaring Twenties and a farewell to old hits. "From now on, I want people to come to my concerts for what I write today, not for what I wrote twenty years ago," he declared at the end of the tour, which was also accompanied by the anthology of the same name.

The Sound+Vision Tour is a jukebox of hits, which brings Bowie back to his full rock-star glory

But the main news, at the start of the '90s, is that Bowie is about to return to being himself in the studio, with a new solo album. It is the seal of a newfound serenity, not only musically. In October 1990, he met Iman Abdulmajid, a Somali-born American top model, one of the first Black models to work with some of the world's biggest fashion houses. It was the hairstylist Teddy Antolin, a mutual friend, who introduced them at a dinner in Los Angeles. "My attraction to her was immediate," he confided. Iman is not convinced that she wants to live with a rock star, but in the end she gives in to his courtship. In April 1992 the two get married in a civil ceremony in Lausanne, and in June in a religious ceremony in the American Episcopal Church of Saint James in Florence. The reception at Villa La Massa, in the Tuscan countryside, includes Valentino, Yoko Ono, and Bono Vox among the guests. The couple settles in New York. David will confide that marrying Iman is the greatest success of his life. From that love, in 2000, his daughter, Alexandria Zahra, was born.

David Bowie smiles alongside his future wife, Iman, in Paris during the premiere of Anima Mundi, *September 9, 1991.*

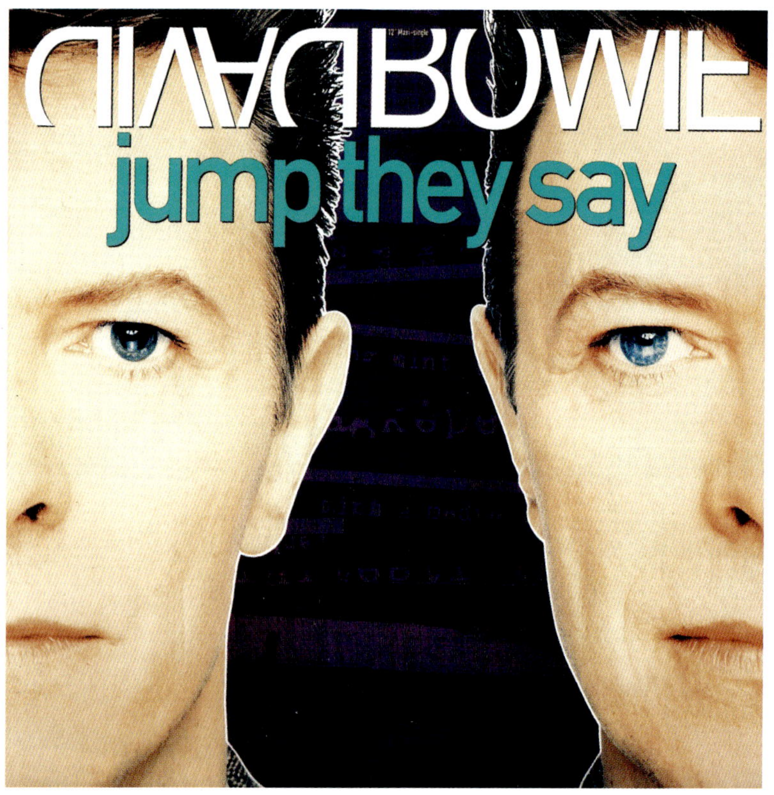

The euphoria of a fresh marriage permeates the grooves of the new LP, *Black Tie White Noise*. Two tracks—the instrumental "The Wedding," the soundtrack of the ceremony that suggestively blends the atmospheres of the two rites (Protestant and Muslim), and the sung version "The Wedding Song"—are dedicated to Iman. Bowie's creativity is also rekindled by the newfound partnership with Nile Rodgers, who coproduces the album with him. This time, however, in the sessions between Montreux and New York, he does not ask him for new hits, but only to work his magic on songs that must possess a marked experimental vein. And where the synergy between the two is ignited, the results are visible. Starting with the single "Jump They Say," which, despite the enthralling funk-rock pace (with solo by the legendary trumpeter Lester Bowie), recalls a tragic biographical starting point, the death of his beloved brother Terry, who committed suicide under a train on January 16, 1985, after being hospitalized for years in London's Cane Hill psychiatric hospital. In the video, directed by Mark Romanek, Bowie plays a civil servant who leans out from the ledge of a building and crashes into a car in the street. It's a symbolic snapshot: out with the glossy dreams and pop colors of the '80s, in with harshness and violence: the aesthetics of the new decade are defined. Also reconnecting the threads with the past is the presence of two old friends, called to perform the instrumental solos on "Looking for Lester" and on the cover of Cream's *I Feel Free*: pianist Mike Garson (last present on *Young Americans*) and guitarist Mick Ronson, in his first appearance since *Pinups* and, unfortunately, his last musical performance: He died of liver cancer on April 29, 1993, a few days after the album's release.

Above: The cover of the single "Jump They Say" (1993)
Right: David Bowie on the set of the music video for "Jump They Say" in Los Angeles, March 1993

A hybrid of black-and-white content right from the title, *Black Tie White Noise* delves into the reality of new social conflicts in America, with harsh insights into racism and urban violence, as in the title track, an unusual hip-hop duet with Al B. Sure!, inspired by the 1992 revolt in the Black ghetto of Los Angeles. The sound attempts to refresh the pan-European modernism of the Berlin trilogy with gusts of free jazz that go well with what Bowie had already experimented with in terms of harmonic disarticulation on albums such as *Lodger* and *Scary Monsters*. House, jazz, rock, and soul thus become the coordinates of a new attempt to define "modern dance." What is lacking, if anything, are the refrains, the characteristic hooks of the best Bowie songbook. But its oblique attitude, which permeates tracks such as the electronic "Nite Flights," a cover of a Walker Brothers gem, "You've Been Around" (again with Gabrels's contribution), the mantra of "Pallas Athena" (also released as a 45 rpm for clubs under the pseudonym *Tao Jones Index*), and "Don't Let Me Down & Down" (a remake of an African ballad dear to Iman), makes it the perfect springboard for the subsequent and more convincing efforts of the '90s. Bowie himself will experience the project as a liberation: "The passage of time has brought maturity and the desire to abandon full control over my emotions, to let them go a little, to start entering into relationships with others," he will confide to *Rolling Stone*.

Bowie also becomes the godfather of the new Britpop scene, starting with the new glam of Suede

Having regained a good feeling with the critics (thanks to the best reviews he has received in the past ten years), Bowie enters the new decade with the moral authority of the godfather (also) of the new Britpop generation, led by bands such as Blur, Oasis, Pulp, and Suede. The latter, in particular, openly acknowledged the debt of their sound, which echoed the melodramatic emphasis of glam: "We stole a lot of things from you; for example, the low-octave voice and things like that that make the songs darker," leader Brett Anderson admitted in a double interview with his idol to NME, in which the two exchanged compliments. Curiously, it was the eponymous *Suede* that *Black Tie White Noise* would knock off the top of the UK Chart, a triumphant return to the track in his homeland that did not correspond to equally favorable results on the other side of the Atlantic, where the album reached only no. 39.

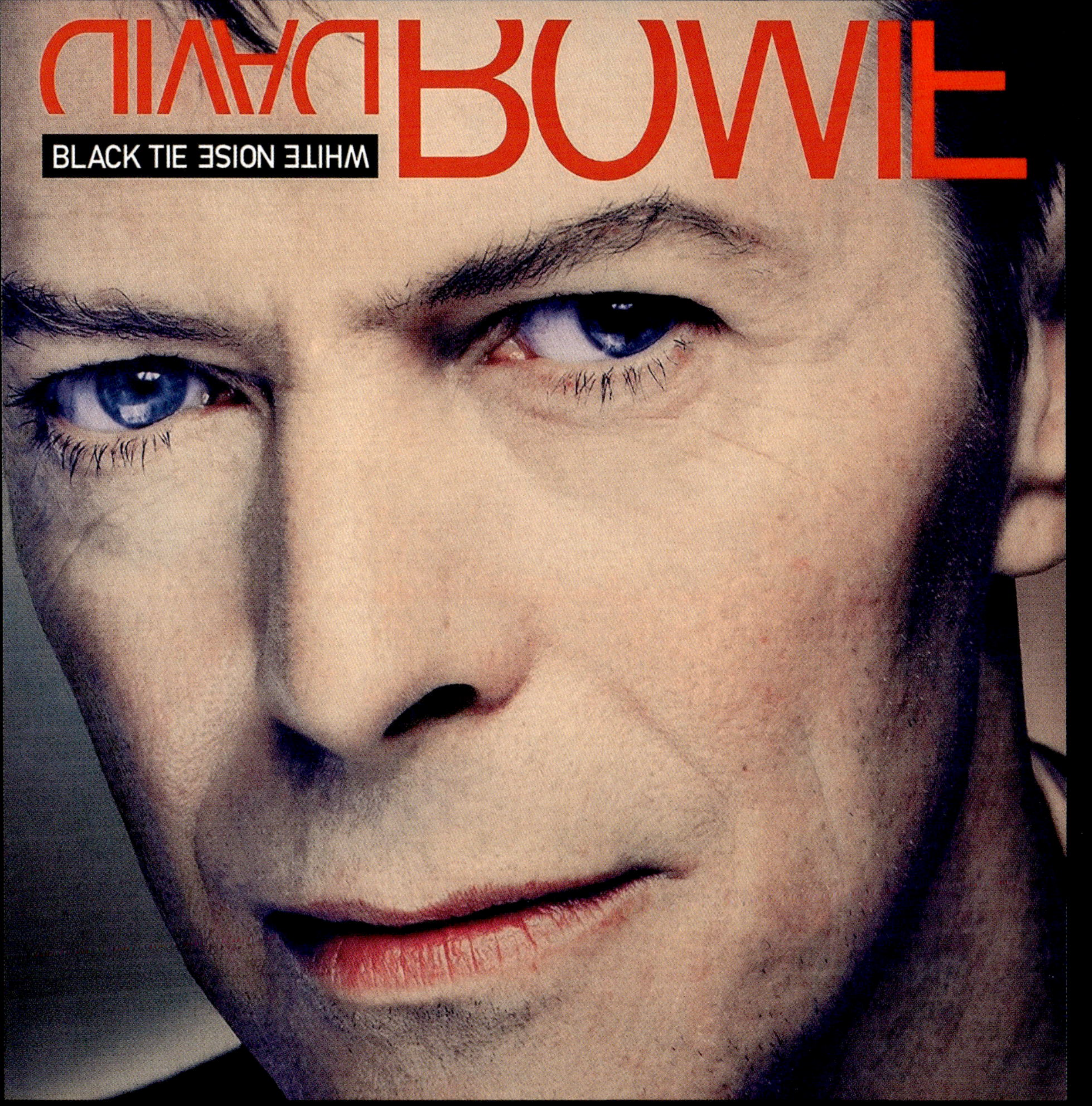

David Bowie on the cover of Black Tie White Noise *(1993), a hybrid album with white-and-black content even in the title*

Confirmation of his newfound experimental verve is also his next project, *The Buddha of Suburbia* (1993), the soundtrack to the TV series of the same title, based on the novel by Anglo-Pakistani writer Hanif Kureishi. A coming-of-age story in which the protagonist Karim, an Anglo-Indian teenager from Bromley, finds his identity amid racial tensions and sexual ambivalence in 1970s London, establishing himself as an actor, while his father discovers he is a suburban Buddhist guru and his friend Charlie becomes a rock star. Halfway between social satire and philosophical analysis, the story strikes Bowie, who cannot help but find analogies with his own personal story, as well as themes that have always interested him, including his never-ending attraction to Buddhism.

The title track, "Buddha of Suburbia," is conceived as a pastiche of Bowie's '70s repertoire, with autobiographical nuances enclosed between such lines as "Englishmen going insane" and "Screaming along in south London, vicious but ready to learn." This will actually be the only track present in the TV film, while the rest of the track list will form a fully autonomous work.

Flirting with pop, jazz, and ambient, the English artist is also at ease as a multi-instrumentalist, supported by Kizilcay, Garson, and guitarist Lenny Kravitz (in the alternative version of the title track). The result is an intriguing collection oscillating between pounding dance rhythms ("Sex and the Church") and art rock numbers ("Dead Against It" and the first version of "1.Outside's Strangers When We Meet"); suggestive instrumental panels, such as the free number "South Horizon," with Garson's improvisation on the piano and the scratches of Bowie's sax; the rarefied flashes of "The Mysteries" and that cosmic soup of sounds that is Ian Fish, UK Heir, later taken up in the documentary *Moonage Daydream* by Brett Morgen (2022).

Although Bowie listed it among his favorite albums, *The Buddha of Suburbia* would have an unfortunate fate. "It was cataloged as a soundtrack, unfit to generate revenue, so it had zero promotion: a disgrace!" he would denounce.

Left: David Bowie during the interview for the Japanese newspaper Asahi Shimbun, *in Tokyo, May 12, 1990*
Above: The cover of The Buddha of Suburbia *(1993), conceived as the soundtrack for the BBC TV series of the same title*

Above: David Bowie and one of his paintings at the Eduard Nakhamkin Fine Arts Gallery in New York
Right: The cover of 1.Outside*, the album that seals the return of Brian Eno, released in 1995*

In the meantime, Bowie devotes himself to the most-varied interests, starting with his passion for art, which he had cultivated since the 1970s, after meeting Andy Warhol at the legendary Factory in New York, and which in the 1990s led him to exhibit in some English galleries, starting with his first solo show, *New Afro/Pagan and Work: 1975–1995* at the Cork Street Gallery in London. His painting, explains the Imago website, "is violent and material, of expressionist origin, in the wake of the works of Ernst Ludwig Kirchner, to the point of recalling art brut and the language of Jean Michel Basquiat." He also collaborates as an editorialist with the magazine *Modern Painters*. "Art is a continuous nourishment," he confided to the *New York Times* in 1998: "It conditions my state of mind. The same work can influence me in different ways, depending on how I approach it." It was during these years that he began to grow his collection, dedicated largely to British art but also to various other schools, often unconventional, as in the case of Gugging, a group of psychiatric

patients who had created therapeutic works. After Bowie's death in 2016, his collection of over 400 works would be auctioned for 41 million Euros. To seal the newfound creative fervor comes his '90s musical masterpiece, the fruit of the long-awaited return to the company of Brian Eno. The "nonmusician" had been struck by the sounds of *The Buddha of Suburbia*, in which he recognized the talent of the Berlin era, fifteen years after the last collaboration of *Lodger*. When the two meet again at Mountain Studios, it is as if time hadn't passed. The harmony is reactivated naturally, despite two opposing approaches, described by Bowie as follows: "I am a nineteenth-century type, a born romantic, unlike Brian, who belongs to the end of the twentieth century. He takes elements of minor art and elevates them to great art, while I do the opposite: I take elements of high art and bring them to the level of street art." Thus the ambitious project of *1.Outside* took shape, conceived as the first chapter of a series of concept albums that, however, never saw completion. This time also in the role of producer along with Bowie himself and Richards, Eno deals the cards of his "Oblique Strategies" to a lineup that is almost a "best of" the musicians who had been joining the court of the Thin White Duke over the years: In addition to Alomar (rhythm guitar), Garson (piano), and Kızılçay (bass, keyboards), there are the drummer Sterling Campbell of Soul Asylum (already behind the drums for *Black Tie White Noise*) and the former Tin Machine Reeves Gabrels on lead guitar, as well as Kevin Armstrong, last heard on that band's second LP.

But the real conductor is a revitalized Bowie, who sings, plays (saxophone, guitar, and keyboards), designs the cover (an acrylic self-portrait on canvas, titled *Head of DB*), and crowds the album's plot with ideas, stories, and characters.

The narrative device is a highly disturbing story: Detective Nathan Adler, of the art crimes section, investigates the murder of Baby Grace Blue, a fourteen-year-old killed and mutilated in an extreme body-art performance. Involved in the investigation are some shady characters: Leon Blank, a mixed-race man with a criminal record for plagiarism; Algeria Touchshriek, a trafficker in art drugs and genetic imprints; the informant Paddy; and Ramona A. Stone, a creator of jewelry made from human parts, as well as a drug dealer. Looming over them all is the menacing presence of the Artist/Minotaur, lurking behind the ritual artistic murder: a dark and grotesque drama, in which Bowie's new obsessions for extreme body art intertwines with the internet and cyberpunk aesthetics (a year later, David Cronenberg's *Crash,* inspired by the novel of the same title by James Graham Ballard, will be released in theaters). We are in full "Pre-Millennium Tension," to quote Tricky. And who better than the one who had always considered that time, a merciless constant of human existence, could take charge of it? As if the dystopian Hunger City had materialized in that last glimpse of the twentieth century. "The fact of placing the disturbing environment of a Diamond Dogs city in the '90s gave it a completely different movement," explained Bowie, interpreting the anguish of "what would happen now, not tomorrow" from the title track, while "the twentieth century dies" from "I Have Not Been to Oxford Town."

In addition to the fascination with the most-extreme fringes of performance art, the work is informed by a sort of new paganism, which to Bowie appears to be a "surrogate for the spiritual hunger in circulation." All this is read from the perspective of the outsider relegated to the margins of society. Here, then, are lyrics imbued with a sense of death ("but the will to live is dead" . . . "This chaos is killing me") and frost ("Cold winter bleeds on the girders of

Babel"), in which the loss of faith ("Don't tell God your plans / It's all deranged") is associated with an attraction to crime, a symptom of a rotting world ("Blended sunrise / and it's a dying world"), in which murder and the mutilation of bodies have become the latest trend of a degenerate art form. But the narrative path is chaotic, the result of an exaggerated cutup technique by Bowie, through the digital tool of the Verbasizer, a program for randomly juxtaposing words.

Musically, it is a catalog of the coolest sounds of the decade, from trip-hop to techno, passing through the abrasive industrial of Trent Reznor's Nine Inch Nails, who a year earlier had released the epochal and no less morbid *The Downward Spiral*. The perfect example is the art rock of the single "The Hearts Filthy Lesson," accompanied by a video full of references to the disturbing body art of Hermann Nitsch, in an orgy of dismembered and reassembled mannequins, set in a warehouse-atelier. It is the macabre backdrop to the ritual murder of Baby Grace Blue, propelled by obsessive rhythms and marred by distorted guitars and industrial clangs: Not by chance, it was chosen for the soundtrack of the cult thriller *Seven* by David Fincher of the same year. A cinematic destiny shared by another noir-tinged track, the desolate "I'm Deranged," whose visionary charge will not escape a master of the genre like David Lynch, who will use it in his very disturbing *Lost Highway* from 1997, almost as if to close the circle of crossed references, if we consider the TV series *Twin Peaks* among the album's innumerable sources of inspiration. And while the majestic *Outside* brings us back to more-enveloping sounds, with airy singing à la Walker, galactic storms punctuate the Stardustesque echo of "Hallo Spaceboy," pierced by Gabrels's guitar slashes (it will be accompanied by a clip by Mallet and remixed in a dance key by the Pet Shop Boys), and a ritual sense inspires robotic funk hybrids such as "I Have Not Been to Oxford Town," "Thru' These Architects Eyes," and "No Control," a sort of reprise of the title track in its futuristic and apocalyptic pace.

On the more experimental side, however, are the devilish industrial "The Voyeur of Utter Destruction," the alienating "A Small Plot of Land," and the claustrophobic "Wishful Beginnings," written with Eno, which combines rarefied sounds with a dramatic text, with sadism tempered by sweetness, a widespread feeling among killers toward their victims, with the request for an apology ("sorry, little girl") that sounds as chilling as the self-indulgence of the key phrase "We had such wishful beginnings / But we lived unbearable lives."

And if the monologues of the concept's protagonists sharpen the sense of alienation, the tension is eased by the melancholic jazz-club nuances of the love song "The Motel" and the fatalistic reflection of "Strangers When We Meet," a reworking of the track already present in *The Buddha of Suburbia:* It is the epilogue of a collection of nineteen songs for almost seventy-five minutes of music, the longest in Bowie's discography.

Published with the subtitle *The Ritual Art-Murder of Baby Grace Blue: A non-linear Gothic Drama Hyper-Cycle*, complete with "Nathan Adler's Diary" included in the booklet, *1.Outside* is another magnificent shot from Bowie to the critics, who, despite some appreciation, will struggle to find a thread in his overflowing ideas. Moreover, at the opening of the film *Moonage Daydream*, right on the hammering cadences of "Hallo Spaceboy," the Thin White Duke explains how chaos has always been a stylistic feature of his work and that he perceived the '90s as particularly chaotic and fragmented. It is no coincidence that "Hallo Spaceboy" itself says, "Do you like girls or boys? / It's confusing these days / But moondust will cover you . . . / This chaos is killing me." Over time, however, *1.Outside* would be recognized as a classic. It would also achieve a fair amount of success in the charts, reaching no. 8 in the UK and no. 20 in the US. If we were to see a sinister omen in it, *1.Outside* also represents the first embryo of that idea of death as an artistic work that the Starman would lucidly apply to himself twenty years later, with the spectacular epitaph of *Blackstar*.

The work of art is complete only when the public adds its own interpretation to it.

DAVID BOWIE

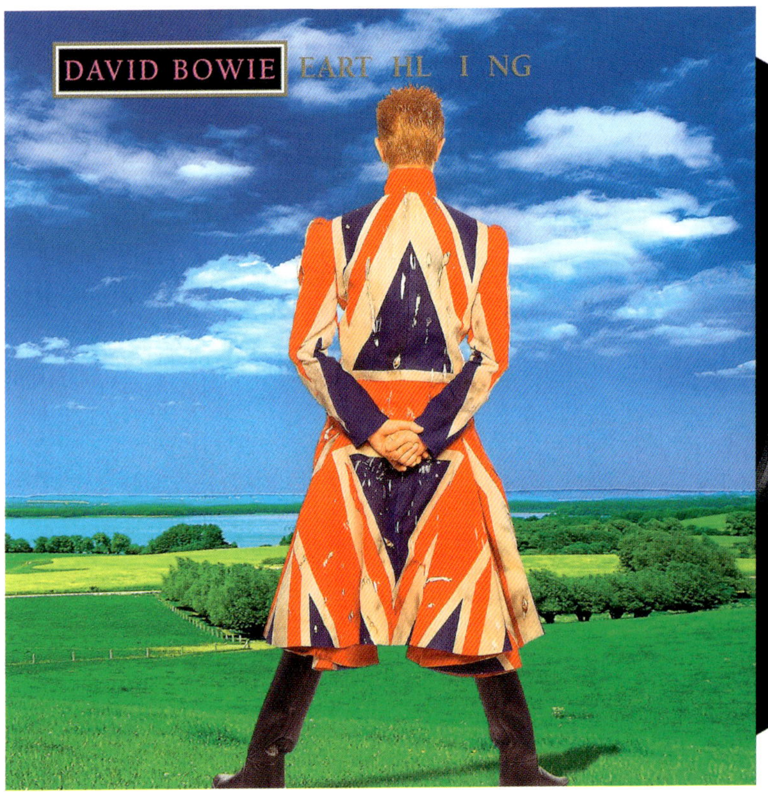

look has also changed: the long blond hair of the late '80s has been replaced by a short cut with a thin goatee and earring, more in line with the times. Just as tuned to the most-popular sound waves of the period is the sound of the new album, produced by the Thin White Duke himself together with the New Yorker Mark Plati, already alongside Prince in *Graffiti Bridge*, and the now- inseparable Gabrels. Instead of riding the nostalgic wave of a return to the past, Bowie goes against the current and dives into a new sound universe, that of underground clubs, marked by the frenetic rhythms of jungle, drum and bass, and breakbeat, with artists such as Tricky, Goldie, and Prodigy in the rearview mirror. "I was attracted to those rhythms," he will say. "I found them very exciting, like every new rhythm that is about to become the language of its time. We wanted to juxtapose all the dance styles we worked with live: jungle, aggressive rock, and industrial stuff." It's as if the techno experiments of *1.Outside* were spun at maximum speed. And the sessions in New York also flow quickly, at the Looking Glass studio owned by Philip Glass, in the company of the band assembled for the *1.Outside* tour, in which, in addition to the faithful Garson and Gabrels, the new bassist Gail Ann Dorsey and the drummer Zachary Alford stand out.

But the second chapter of "Nathan Adler Diaries" will never see the light. Because Bowie, in the meantime, has already landed elsewhere, ensnared by the call of the jungle. It's time for new end-of-the-millennium cutups to the frenetic rhythm of *Earthling*, the album in which the ex-alien becomes terrestrial. On the cover, he is shown from behind, wearing a flashy frock coat with the Union Jack (by Alexander McQueen), almost as if he wanted to claim the moral paternity of that Cool Britannia that is raging across the Channel thanks to the new phenomenon of Britpop. His

Above: Bowie, his back turned to us, wears a flamboyant redingote featuring the Union Jack (by Alexander McQueen), on the cover of Earthling *(1997).*
Right: A portrait of Bowie in 1997

Written and recorded in just two weeks, *Earthling* is preceded by a new twist: the online launch, as a free download, of the electrifying "Telling Lies." Gabrels's sharp guitars and Garson's jazz piano engage in a furious hand-to-hand combat with a rhythm section that runs wildly on a synthetic background where the most-disparate samples swarm, a babel of sounds and rhythms that will lend itself well to the numerous future remixes. Here then are dance-floor sonic assaults, like the other single "Little Wonder," which mixes rock riffs and jungle blasts with Bowie's frenetic singing, the drum and bass-jazz-rock hybrid of "Battle for Britain (The Letter)," in which the free piano of *Aladdin Sane* resurfaces behind a wall of layered polyrhythms, the pressing electronic hard pop of *Dead Man Walking*, propelled by drum-machine loops and closed by new jazz-piano phrases, and the electronic apotheosis of "Law (Earthlings on Fire)" between alien synths and filtered voice.

But the patchwork of *Earthling* is not a vain pursuit of the latest fashion, as many will superficially theorize, making Bowie furious: "I hate the fact that the impression is spread that it is only about jungle. The record owes something to drum and bass for the use of rhythm, but the result is light-years away from what Goldie or any other standard-bearer of that genre could do." In fact, the Thin White Duke's rock vision remains

I'M AFRAID OF AMERICANS TARGETS THE OBTUSITY OF CONSUMER SOCIETY, SYMBOLIZED BY JOHNNY, THE AVERAGE AMERICAN

central, permeating episodes such as "Looking for Satellites," with hypnotic bass, hieratic singing, and a derailing guitar solo; the vibrant funky invective of "I'm Afraid of Americans" (taken from the *1.Outside* sessions); and the mysticism of "Seven Years in Tibet," the emotional climax of the album, which alternates an indolent bluesy pace with thunderous industrial walls of distorted guitars, culminating in the ecstatic hymn of the refrain: "I praise to you / Nothing ever goes away."

The lyrics also reopen social and spiritual meditations that have always been dear to the English artist, reflecting on the difficult universal condition of man ("Looking for Satellites," "Dead Man Walking") and criticizing the obtuseness of consumer society, symbolized by Johnny, the average American protagonist of "I'm Afraid of Americans," who proclaims "God is an American," renewing transoceanic fears at the age of twenty-two since "Young Americans." "Seven Years in Tibet" instead addresses the consolidated interest in Buddhism, denouncing the oppression of the Tibetan people by China, narrating the story of the killing of a monk, inspired by the book of the same name by Heinrich Harrer, which Jean-Jacques Annaud would adapt to the big screen a few months later. Translated into Mandarin, "Seven Years in Tibet" would become the last no. 1 in the Hong Kong charts before the return to Chinese control in June 1997.

For the occasion, Bowie also shows off some of his best videos of the '90s. Starting with "Little Wonder," directed by the Italian Canadian Floria Sigismondi, with hyperkinetic editing: The protagonists are a series of Ziggy Stardust clones who wander around a cyberpunk London, while zoomorphic puppets and images of agitated faces appear, curated by the artist Tony Oursler, who will also collaborate on the staging of the *Earthling* tour. Sigismondi repeats herself with "Dead Man Walking," where, at the usual infernal rhythm, citations by the painter Francis Bacon follow one another in a blood-red blaze, with bassist Gail Ann Dorsey transformed into a grotesque satyr figure; while in the paranoid video for "I'm Afraid of Americans," directed by Dom and Nic, a terrified Bowie is chased through the streets of New York by Trent Reznor, in the guise of a character similar to Robert De Niro in *Taxi Driver*.

More compact and immediate than its predecessor, *Earthling* will once again intrigue critics and will obtain good commercial results (no. 6 in the UK), also thanks to a massive promotion.

As a consummate self-manager, the Thin White Duke listed his "Bowie bonds" on the stock exchange. The scheme involved a particular form of bond, securitizations with a guarantee deriving from the proceeds of twenty-five albums. The bonds were bought en masse by an insurance company, Prudential Insurance, for fifty-five million dollars. And Bowie used the money he earned to acquire the rights to his other songs. The money machine will jam when online music opens a loophole in copyright legislation, with a consequent market crisis, which will cause the bonds to collapse, reducing them to (star)dust. So in 2007 the bonds will be liquidated and the rights will return to Bowie. But it is not the only financial operation of the English artist's time, who goes so far as to create his own virtual bank: Bowie Bank customers have ATMs and checks with the man's effigy, even though it is another bank, USABancShares.com, that manages the depositors' money. Already the following year, however, Bowie Bank will be only a faint memory. His are all ephemeral actions, which nevertheless testify to the insatiable curiosity, as well as the new passion for the internet, which will yield innovative projects on the BowieNet website.

Meanwhile, the Thin White Duke had reached the age of fifty, which he celebrated with a stellar party on January 9, 1997, at Madison Square Garden in New York. In addition to previewing several songs from *Earthling*, Bowie welcomed onstage friends and colleagues such as Dave Grohl (Foo Fighters), Billy Corgan (Smashing Pumpkins), Frank Black (Pixies), Kim Gordon and Thurston Moore of Sonic Youth, Robert Smith of the Cure, with whom he created the poignant "Quicksand," and Lou Reed, with whom he launched into a revisitation of Velvet Underground classics such as "I'm Waiting for the Man" and "White Light / White Heat." A group photo portrayed them all excited and enthusiastic about finding themselves at the court of the Thin White Duke, who revealed to the *New York Daily News* that "I never expected, at my age, to have such a hunger for life. I thought, like all great romantic heroes, I had given everything. But nothing has changed. I still feel charged." Titled *David Bowie and Friends: A Very Special Concert*, the show will be broadcast on pay-per-view in the US, with proceeds going to Save the Children.

"I thought, like all great romantic heroes, I had given my all. But I still feel charged," Bowie revealed on his fiftieth birthday.

The former space boy thus remains faithful to the Wildian imperative of "life as a work of art," perpetuating his drive to constantly turn the page. If a criticism could be made of daring operations such as *1.Outside* and *Earthling*, it is that of attempting to chase, for once, sounds that were already established and in vogue at the time. So, what could be the most disconcerting new move? Go back twenty-eight years, reembracing a more traditional melodic sensibility, in an ideal sequel to *Hunky Dory*.

David Bowie blows on the candles for his fiftieth birthday during a concert/event at Madison Square Garden in New York on January 9, 1997.

This is the intent behind *Hours . . .*, Bowie's last LP of the century, released by Virgin in 1999. Unfortunately, however, very few songs can be compared to the 1971 masterpiece. Written and produced together with Gabrels and recorded at Seaview Studios in Bermuda, the tracks on *Hours . . .* are permeated by a nostalgic spell, with an eye to when guitar and voice were enough to make songs take off into space. "The album," Bowie will explain, "is about a man who looks back and retraces his life. That's why I wanted to give a sign of how I wrote songs before." And again: "I wanted to capture that kind of universal restlessness felt by many people my age. I'm trying to write songs for my generation." A feeling symbolized by the "sacred" image on the cover, in which, in the classic pose of the Pietà, a young Bowie holds the Bowie of today in his arms. And it is precisely the passing of time, the theme of the single "Thursday's Child," or rather the ancient Bowian melody ferried toward the year 2000 in a melancholic ballad. Rarely, however, does the rest of the set list reach such heights. Among the best episodes, the rock ballad "Something in the Air," with distorted vocals and accompanying feedback; the hypnotic "If I'm Dreaming My Life," where an acid guitar acts as a counterpoint to the dreamy singing; and the oriental folk of "Seven." Elsewhere, Gabrels's guitar overlays almost seem to suffocate the songs, which do not find the freshness of the glam era ("What's Really Happening?," "The Pretty Things Are Going to Hell," "New Angels Of Promise").

Bowie performs onstage at the Astoria, London, December 2, 1999, during the Hours . . . tour. It was his last album of the twentieth century, released in 1999.

Despite reaching fifth place in the UK Chart, *Hours . . .* will not leave its mark, but it remains a sincere testimony to the desire to rediscover more-intimate and reflective atmospheres, including a renewed spiritual vein, which is reflected in the cover image itself, as well as in the lyrics. The Thin White Duke closes the century that consecrated him as a global star with the Hours Tour. In the meantime, director Todd Haynes immortalized him in *Velvet Goldmine* (1998), a portrait of the glam season—but without his songs, which Bowie, in disagreement with the distorted vision of his figure, refused to grant, confirming, once again, the desire to maintain maximum control over his artistic management, an approach that will be reaffirmed

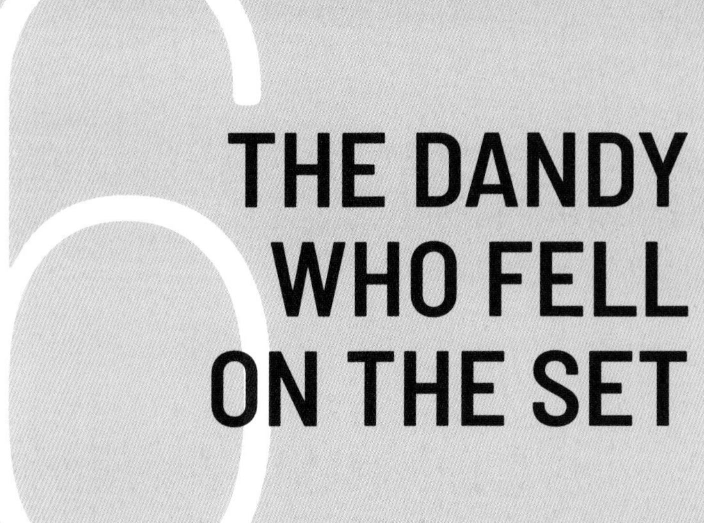

6 THE DANDY WHO FELL ON THE SET

ADVENTURES ON THE BIG SCREEN: A NEW GALLERY OF CHARACTERS

If Bowie's musical career was a constant metamorphosis of styles and masks, no less varied was the gallery of characters and genres that saw him as a protagonist in cinema: a natural habitat, that of a cinema set, for a multimedia artist who has always made the visual component an essential ingredient of his multifaceted work.

A versatile actor, capable of ranging from comedy to horror, from science fiction to war films

In total, the London dandy has participated in about twenty feature films, between roles and cameos, ranging from science fiction to comedy, from drama to fantasy, from horror to war films.

After a few small experiments, his real cinematic debut can be traced back to 1976, when the English director Nicolas Roeg hired him as the protagonist of *The Man Who Fell to Earth,* based on the novel of the same title by Walter Travis. Bowie plays Thomas Jerome Newton, an alien who landed on Earth in search of water, who, thanks to his superior technological knowledge, founds a financial empire and designs a spaceship to return to his planet. But he will have to deal with humans. . . .

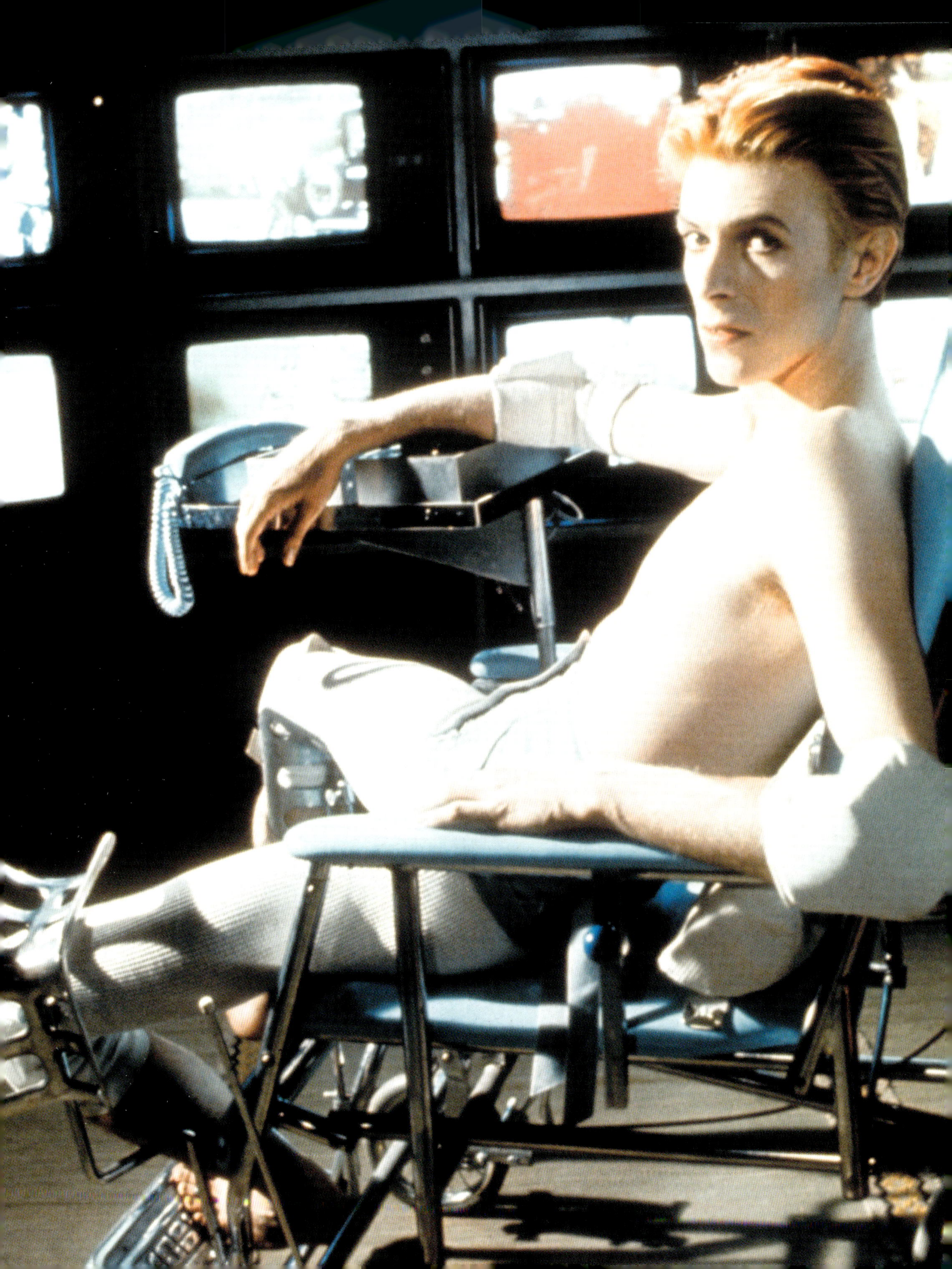

The former Ziggy Stardust—at the time fully addicted to cocaine—appears pale and very thin, with a lost and detached look. His alienated reality is mirrored in that of the protagonist, for a visionary film made of desaturated colors and bare settings, in which, among other things, themes often at the center of Bowie's songbook emerge (the sense of alienation, life in space, the power of television, loneliness). Underrated at the time of its release, the film will become a cult classic, also inspired by the TV series of the same title by Alex Kurtzman, with some iconic images, such as the one in which Bowie sits in a room surrounded by monitors. And the character of the Thin White Duke himself will show more than one affinity with this emaciated and cold alien fallen to Earth.

If Roeg's film played on the early Bowie's identification with science fiction and his alien aspect, in the following *Gigolo* (1978) the director David Hemmings tried to exploit his interest at the time for the Berlin of the Weimar Republic, setting there the story of a Prussian veteran officer of the First World War who begins to work as a gigolo in a brothel under the service of a baroness, played by Marlene Dietrich, in her last appearance on the screen, in a cast also including Kim Novak and Sydne Rome. It was the presence of Lili Marlene's German muse that convinced Bowie of the project, but the two never crossed paths on set, and the scenes in which they both starred were artfully edited. If for *The Man Who Fell to Earth* Bowie couldn't contribute with the soundtrack, here instead he contributes with a song, "Revolutionary Song," composed with musical director Jack Fishman. The film was not a success, and Bowie commented in his own words by calling it "the 32 Elvis Presley films condensed into one."

The fascination with Berlin in the late '70s will push him to another foray on the set, this time in the guise of himself: the messianic appearance in *Christiane F.—We Children from Bahnhof Zoo* by Ulrich Edel, in the famous concert scene, with a spectacular interpretation of "Station to Station" in front of the wide-eyed young Christiane (Natja Brunckhorst) and her friends.

Previous page and left: David Bowie as the alien Thomas Newton in the sci-fi film The Man Who Fell to Earth *by Nicolas Roeg (1976)*
Above: The poster for the film Gigolo *(1978) by David Hemmings, which, alongside Bowie, starred Marlene Dietrich in her last appearance on screen*

David Bowie as the vampire John, with Catherine Deneuve in a scene from The Hunger (1983) by Tony Scott

But it was above all in the following decade that Bowie's cinematic career took off, thanks in particular to two films from 1983: *The Hunger* by the Englishman Tony Scott, and *Merry Christmas, Mr. Lawrence* (*Furyo*) by the Japanese Nagisa Oshima.

In the first, based on the novel of the same title by Whitley Strieber, along with a Mephistophelian Catherine Deneuve, he forms a couple of metropolitan vampires (Miriam and John Blaylock) who may have been remembered thirty years later by Jim Jarmusch's *Only Lovers Left Alive* (2013). It is a dark and aestheticized portrait of New York in the early '80s, at the service of a sensual horror story, in which a young Susan Sarandon also bursts in as the frigid doctor Sarah Roberts. Bowie, in the role of the emaciated John, who wastes away quickly without being able to find lifeblood even in his victims, still has to deal with his personal *Picture of Dorian Gray*, while the gothic setting favors the meeting with his Bauhaus disciples, who put their chilling "Bela Lugosi Is Dead" at the center of the soundtrack.

Even more successful is his performance in *Furyo*, where the role of the New Zealand officer Jack Celliers guarantees him one of the best performances of his career. The film brings together the talent of Oshima—the director who had reinvented eroticism in Japan with *In the Realm of the Senses* (1976)—the ambiguous charm of a platinum-haired Bowie and the musical genius of Ryuichi Sakamoto, who composed the legendary main theme (the splendid "Forbidden Colors," with lyrics and performance by David Sylvian) as well as playing the ruthless Captain Yonoi, head of a prison camp in Java in 1942. Against the backdrop of the eternal clash of cultures, a game of power and seduction takes place that culminates in the famous scene of Celliers's sacrifice: His kiss to the petrified Yonoi will reveal the unspeakable homosexual passion of his tormentor, sealing the fate of both. A sort of extreme triumph of love, in all its shades, over the brutality of war and human conventions. It is probably the best film of Bowie's acting career, even if the scene is often stolen by the other protagonist, Tom Conti, and by a legendary Takeshi Kitano, especially in the memorable finale.

Bowie is featured alongside Ryuichi Sakamoto in the poster for the film Furyo *by Nagisa Oshima (1983).*

After a cameo in Dianne Jackson's charming animated short *The Snowman*, based on Raymond Briggs's children's book of the same title, and a minor role as the bizarre hitman Colin Morris in John Landis's *Into the Night* (1985), Bowie returned to the set for Julien Temple's *Absolute Beginners* (1986), bringing with him the nostalgic main song that would survive well beyond the film's (rather short) breath. In the story, based on Colin MacInnes's book of the same name that narrates London in the late 1950s, among jazz, ambitious girls, and race riots, he has a minor, but rather incisive, role as the megalomaniac advertising executive Vendice Partners. However, that will not be enough—despite the presence of singers who were on the rise at the time, such as Sade and Patsy Kensit—to redeem the film's failure. The soundtrack, which will feature contributions from the protagonists, Style Council, Ray Davies, and Gil Evans, will work better.

Above: David Bowie with Patsy Kensit and Eddie O'Connell in the poster of Absolute Beginners, *the musical by Julien Temple (1986)*
Right: Bowie as Jareth, the king of Goblins, in the poster for the fantasy film Labyrinth *(1986), directed by Jim Henson*

Among the most-bizarre Bowie cinematic incarnations, there is certainly Jareth the Goblin King, the ruler with the long blonde mop at the center of the fantasy *Labyrinth* (1986). Directed by Jim Henson, the creator of the Muppets, the film sees a teenager, Jennifer Connelly, grappling with a fairy-tale world, populated by humans and puppets, in which the evil Jareth kidnaps her little brother, ensnaring her for a long time with his magic tricks, before the reassuring happy ending. After a lukewarm reception, the film will gradually become a cult classic: Not by chance in 2025, the news of a sequel arrived, entrusted to Robert Eggers, the ambitious director of *The Lighthouse* and *Nosferatu*.

In some ways even more surprising was Bowie's participation two years later in Martin Scorsese's *The Last Temptation of Christ*, in the role of a glacial Pontius Pilate, intent on interrogating the tormented and dark Jesus played by Willem Dafoe. Legend has it that "with true rock-star timing," Bowie shot his sequence in a single day.

JIM HENSON, GEORGE LUCAS AND DAVID BOWIE
TAKE YOU INTO A DAZZLING WORLD OF FANTASY AND ADVENTURE.

LABYRINTH

Where everything seems possible and nothing is what it seems.

HENSON ASSOCIATES, INC. AND LUCASFILM LTD. PRESENT A JIM HENSON FILM DAVID BOWIE JENNIFER CONNELLY "LABYRINTH" Executive Producer GEORGE LUCAS
Directed by JIM HENSON Conceptual Design by BRIAN FROUD Story by DENNIS LEE and JIM HENSON Screenplay by TERRY JONES Score by TREVOR JONES Executive Supervising Producer DAVID LAZER Produced by ERIC RATTRAY
Director of Photography ALEX THOMSON, B.S.C. Production Designer ELLIOT SCOTT Special Effects Supervisor GEORGE GIBBS Editor JOHN GROVER With Creatures Performed by DAVID GOELZ · STEVE WHITMIRE · KAREN PRELL
RON MUECK · KEVIN CLASH · SHARI WEISER · ANTHONY ASBURY · BRIAN HENSON AND FRANK OZ

PG PARENTAL GUIDANCE SUGGESTED
SOME MATERIAL MAY NOT BE SUITABLE FOR CHILDREN

DOLBY STEREO

NOVEL FROM HENRY HOLT & Co

DELPHI

ORIGINAL SOUNDTRACK ALBUM AVAILABLE ON EMI AMERICA RECORDS AND CASSETTES

TRI-STAR

Less relevant, all things considered, are his forays on the set in the '90s. Richard Shepard's *The Linguini Incident* (1991), which sees him as the protagonist alongside Rosanna Arquette in the role of a bartender hunting for a green card, is remembered above all for the cameos of his future wife, Iman, and the singer-songwriter Julian Lennon. Still on the comedy front, certainly not memorable, is his Italian adventure in Giovanni Veronesi's *My West* in the role of the brutal gunslinger Jack Sikora, in a very varied cast also including Leonardo Pieraccioni, Harvey Keitel, and Alessia Marcuzzi. The seasoned gangster in *Everybody Loves Sunshine* (1999), an independent British film directed by Andrew Goth, whose cast included none other than Goldie, with whom Bowie had shared his Jungle and drum and bass skills two years earlier in *Earthling*, also didn't shine.

In Julian Schnabel's *Basquiat*, Bowie gets the chance to play Andy Warhol, one of his masters

And if in the '90s we will also remember a cameo as himself in the TV series *Full Stretch* (1993) and even his transformation into a video game character (in the futuristic *Omikron*), the most convincing interpretation of the decade will remain that of the surreal Andy Warhol in *Basquiat* (1996), a biopic on the life of the famous exponent of neoexpressionism and American writing, in which the director Julian Schnabel brings together a stellar cast (Dennis Hopper, Benicio del Toro, Gary Oldman, Christopher Walken, Willem Dafoe, and Courtney Love).

Left: David Bowie with Rosanna Arquette in the poster for the comedy The Linguini Incident *(1991) by Richard Shepard*
Above, from the left: Bowie (as Andy Warhol), Dennis Hopper, Gary Oldman, and Jeffrey Wright, as Basquiat, in the biopic of the same title

Above and right: David Bowie as Serbian and naturalized American engineer Nikola Tesla in two scenes from The Prestige *(2006) by Christopher Nolan*

Interesting is his experience in the role of FBI special agent Phillip Jeffries, a fictional character from the TV series *Twin Peaks*, created by Mark Frost and David Lynch, where he appears for the first time in the prequel film *Fire Walk with Me* (1992). The character will also be developed in the sequel to the TV series *Twin Peaks—The Return* (2017), but due to Bowie's death, which occurred a year earlier, Jeffries will be represented by puffs of white smoke emitted by a strange machine, similar to a giant teapot, in a motel room. Shortly before dying, Bowie had given Lynch permission to use, in the new series, some clips from the film *Fire Walk with Me* where his character appears, but only on the condition that he be dubbed by an actor originally from Louisiana (!).

With the new millennium, Bowie's film appearances became less frequent, also due to the health problems that had already affected his musical activity. His disturbing Mr. Rice, who after his death leaves a series of clues to a sick twelve-year-old to help him appreciate life, is perhaps the only salient note of

Nicholas Kendall's *Mr. Rice's Secret* (2000), while his cameo as himself in Ben Stiller's *Zoolander* (2001) joins those of a large group of stars (Winona Ryder, Lenny Kravitz, Natalie Portman, Fred Durst, Paris Hilton, and Donald Trump!).

The last notable test on set will therefore be that in *The Prestige* (2006), one of Christopher Nolan's key films, in which Bowie plays the role of Nikola Tesla, a Serbian engineer and physicist who became a naturalized American citizen in the late nineteenth century, who lives in Colorado Springs and helps the magician Robert Angier (Hugh Jackman) build a teleportation machine. Between science and illusion, mystery and mathematics, the English dandy could not be more at ease, with that austere and serene air that he had assumed in the last years of his life.

In a temporal sense, however, David Bowie's last cinematic effort will remain the disturbing cameo in *Land Shark* (August), a 2008 drama film directed by Austin Chick, in which two brothers try to save their Wall Street firm from bankruptcy, a month before the attacks of September 11, 2001.

Then, unfortunately, only the puff of white smoke from the *Twin Peaks* teapot will remain to affectionately remind us of the cinematic parable of a total artist, just like that of David Lynch, who passed away in 2025, with whom we imagine him up there now, intent on conversing about morbid noir atmospheres and refined electronic sounds.

7 THE NEW MILLENNIUM AND THE EPITAPH OF BLACKSTAR

THE STARMAN CHALLENGES DEATH WITH THE MOST SPECTACULAR EXIT

Meanwhile, a new arrival is welcome in the Jones household: on August 15, 2000, Alexandria Zahra is born, the daughter of David and Iman, who do

A NEW ARRIVAL IN THE JONES FAMILY: AMING DAVID AND IMAN ARE PHOTOGRAPHED WITH LITTLE ALEXANDRIA ZAHRA

not hide their happiness by also granting themselves a photo shoot for *Hello!* magazine. Less happy news, however, comes from the upper echelons of Emi/Virgin, which refuses to publish *Toy* (it will be released posthumously, in 2021). Bowie does not take it well. "Terribly hurt" by the decision, he cuts ties with both and creates his own independent label, Iso (abbreviation of the name of his management, Isolar). "Many times I did not agree with how things were done, and I felt frustrated," he explains. "I have dreamed for many years of working with my own structure, and this is the right opportunity."

But even more than the "indie" turn of Iso, which will still operate under the exclusive license of Columbia, what is fueling expectations for the new album is the reunion with Tony Visconti, a good twenty-two years after their last collaboration for *Scary Monsters*. The frost between the two, apparently also caused by the excessive frankness of the producer in some interviews, had actually dissolved some time before, at least since 1998. Visconti will not hide his emotion: "When David got back in touch, I realized how much I missed him. We've both grown up and changed; it was time to resume communication." "Even if we would have remained friends forever, in recent years we hadn't worked together," Bowie will echo. "The new work will mark a critical moment for both of us. But Tony and I have always had the ability to prevent each other from falling into a routine."

It is a thoughtful Bowie, the one in *Heathen*. Influenced by some recent bereavements—the loss of his mother, Peggy, and his friend Freddie Burretti—he questions themes such as faith, death, and the uncertainty of the future, without hiding that typical melancholy that comes when "after fifty you become aware that the time has come to say goodbye to the idea of being young." With the music of Richard Strauss providing new creative stimuli ("There is a universal dimension in the melodies he composed at the end of his life"), he will explain, "I think they are the most terribly romantic, sad, and touching songs that have ever been written."

Recorded between New York and Allaire Studios in the Catskill Mountains, with Alomar and Campbell among the musicians involved, *Heathen* is an album with dark undertones, dominated by an existential fear that filters through from the beginning of the desolate Sunday:

2002

"Nothing remains / We could run when the rain slows / Look for the cars or signs of life," sings a Bowie worried about the future of his daughter, Lexi (*A Better Future*), and for his own life (the title track, defined as "a traumatic epiphany on the awareness of death"). A slow-burning malaise, just like the single "Slow Burn," complete with a poignant melodic opening and piercing guitar by Pete Townshend. It is the emotional peak of the album, together with the touching "Slip Away," in which Bowie returns to play the old Stylophone used in 1969 for *Space Oddity*, in a majestic setting of piano and synthesized strings, to narrate the bitter tale of Floyd Vivino, host of a children's TV show in the '70s.

The other special guest, Dave Grohl of Foo Fighters (ex-Nirvana), performs on the five strings in "I've Been Waiting for You," a reinterpretation of Neil Young's first album that joins the other two covers in the set list: a vibrant "Cactus" by the Pixies, and the homage of "I Took a Trip on a Gemini Spaceship" to Legendary Stardust Cowboy, the bizarre rocker who was an inspiration for Ziggy. Finally, two partially known tracks: "I Would Be Your Slave," performed at Carnegie Hall in New York on February 22, 2002, in the concert for Tibet House, and "Afraid," already shared in 2001 for the Bowienet subscribers.

Heathen (no. 5 in the UK, no. 14 in the USA) shows a mature and thoughtful Bowie, who, although far from the heights of his masterpieces, rediscovers the intensity partially lost in *Hours* . . . . , earning more than one positive review. Visconti, no small part of the creator of the result, will be enthusiastic about it: "I think it's David's magnum opus; it reminds me of a symphony."

Back by his side, producer Tony Visconti praises *Heathen*: "It reminds me of a symphony"

Previous page: David Bowie wearing a frock coat designed by Alexander McQueen at Glastonbury Festival, June 25, 2000

Left: The cover of Heathen*, released in 2002*

STAFF

Left and above: David Bowie performing at the Jones Beach Theater on Long Island, New York, August 2, 2002, during the Heathen tour

In everything I have done, ultimately, there is only one recurring idea: to reflect chaos, to try to organize it.

| DAVID BOWIE

Encouraged by his new recording relationship with Columbia and his newfound friendship with Visconti, Bowie returned to *The Looking Glass Murders* immediately after the end of the Heathen tour. In addition to his longtime producer, he brought back two heavyweights, Mike Garson and Earl Slick, in a team that also included Plati, Campbell, and guitarists David Torn and Gerry Leonard. But the main attraction of *Reality* was its new promotional stunt: an interactive show broadcast via satellite from London's Riverside Studios to eighty-six cinemas in twenty-six countries.

Written and recorded in downtown New York, *Reality* is inevitably affected by the aftermath of the September 11 terrorist attacks and the "irrational feelings you get from living in this city" after those traumatic events. Bowie, however, broadens his horizons, attempting to tell the concept of "reality" and its debasement in Western culture, between political manipulation and media distortions. "Reality has become an abstract concept for many people," he explains to *Sound on Sound*. "What people used to consider truth seems to have vanished. There is nothing left to rely on. Knowledge seems to have been forgotten, and you feel like you are drifting in the middle of the sea." This is also a prescient vision, if you consider that the era of fake news and social media disinformation had yet to come.

Previous pages: David Bowie performing at the Roseland Ballroom in New York, June 11, 2002
Right: The cover of Reality*, released in 2003*

Despite the premises, however, Bowie specifies that this is a more positive album than *Heathen*, going so far as to show a provocative optimism in the Blur-like Britpop of the pressing single "New Killer Star," in which the surreal story of a spaceship that crashes into the heart of America is meant to act as a "reaction to the times we are living in." What is lacking, however, are the sonic intuitions in an album that, beyond a certain newfound aggressiveness, travels for a long time on autopilot, between weak covers (the Spanish-sounding "Pablo Picasso" by Modern Lovers and "Try Some, Buy Some" by the late George Harrison) and retraces of the past, such as "Never Get Old (almost a new "Fame"), the title track (a sort of angry mutation of "Hallo Spaceboy"), the cumbersome soul-funk of "She'll Drive the Big Car," and the atmospheric danceability of "Looking for Water."

So in the end, what hits the mark is the decadent pace of "Bring Me the Disco King," which in its third incarnation (after the aborted versions for *Black Tie White Noise* and *Earthling*) finally finds the right balance thanks to Garson's elegant jazzy nuances.

Despite the undoubted decline in inspiration, *Reality* remained afloat in the charts, especially in Europe (no. 3 in the UK was the best placing since *Black Tie White Noise*), while in the US it stopped at no. 29). But the main attraction was above all the subsequent 2003–2004 tour, with its 121 dates, bringing Bowie back onstage in a series of memorable concerts. Until that dramatic June 25, 2004, when time began to take its toll on him.

As soon as he got off the stage at the Scheessel festival in Germany, Bowie collapsed, two days after the illness that had forced him to interrupt his performance in Prague. Having narrowly avoided a heart attack, he was saved by an angioplasty at the Sankt Georg Hospital in Hamburg. This time he had to give up: He canceled the remaining dates of the tour and entrusted himself to the care of doctors.

Back home for convalescence, in his apartment at 286 Lafayette Street, in the SoHo/Nolita neighborhood of Manhattan, he kept a very low profile. He goes out shopping, takes his daughter to school, and at most attends a one-off gala. In the meantime, the New York rock scene is flourishing with the "nu new wave" with the tormented existentialism of the Strokes and Interpol, which is also taking root on the other side of the Atlantic thanks to Editors, Franz Ferdinand, Bloc Party, and company. It is a common feeling that is rekindled. And a god of that era like the Thin White Duke cannot help but return to the limelight. Groups with obvious elective affinities emerge, such as the New Yorkers TV on the Radio and the Canadians Arcade Fire, which Bowie himself will enthusiastically sponsor: He will lend his voice to the former on Province (on the LP *Return to Cookie Mountain* in 2006), and he will participate in the latter's concert on February 8, 2005, which will also mark his first appearance on a stage since the dramatic evening in Scheessel.

WORLD

MGMT are starting to assert themselves, and they do not fail to acknowledge the crucial influence of the Thin White Duke on their music. And even the one who had been Bowie's harshest critic, Paul Weller, confessed to Mojo in May 2008 that he was now a "converted Bowian." Retrospectives, biographical books, homages, and tributes emerge. But Bowie is no longer in the public eye, except for a sighting at the premiere of his son Duncan's film *Moon* at Sundance in 2010. Thus the wildest rumours are spreading. There are even those who swear that he is close to death.

Previous pages: Two images of David Bowie during a show in preparation for the Reality Tour, *at the club Chance in Poughkeepsie, New York, August 19, 2003.*
Above: The cover of The Next Day *(2013), in which the famous* "Heroes" *picture is covered by a white square with the album title.*

All false. On January 8, 2013, the day of his 66th birthday, Bowie rises again. "Here I am, not quite dying," he announces in "The Next Day," the title track of his new album. Having gathered the partners who accompanied him in the years preceding his disappearance (in addition to Visconti, Slick, Dorsey, Leonard, and Campbell), the English artist throws away all masks, conceiving an intimate, melancholic, painful album. With no more pretenses to hide the wrinkles of time. As in "Where Are We Now?," the single that precedes the album, in which, in the slow progression of a twilight melody, he retraces familiar places with a subdued tone: Potsdamer Platz, Nürnberger Straße, Bösebrücke. . . . Foggy memories of a black-and-white Berlin, emptied of the proud decadence of the hero he once was and filled with a resigned, moving preservation of life. That anguished question, "Where are we now?," remains unresolved. It would almost seem like a farewell, if it weren't for the consoling verses of the finale: "As long as there is sun, as long as there is rain, as long as there is fire, as long as there is me, so that there is you."

But *The Next Day* shows a still-vital Bowie, capable in the title track of dusting off burning rock guitars and a cheeky crooning in keeping with the Berlin times, also evoked by the ironic cover where the historic effigy of *"Heroes"* is defaced by a white box on which the album title stands out. And if *Dirty Boys* also seems to reawaken the sick saxes of decadent Berlin for a fleeting homage to the partnership with Iggy Pop, the single "The Stars (Are Out Tonight)" makes its way through hallucinatory riffs with an epic chorus and a bridge that winks at Roxy Music's "If There Is Something"—already covered in the days of Tin Machine, whose metallic crashes resonate in "(You Will) Set The World on Fire"—and the robotic psychedelia of "How Does the Grass Grow?" takes off on a pressing incipit à la "Boys Keep Swinging," showing off a chorus modeled on "Apache" by the Shadows.

With the persuasive pop of *Valentine's Day*, caressing glam tones re-emerge to hide the harshness of the text, inspired by the drama of the massacres in American schools, while "If You Can See Me" recovers drum and bass impulses à la *Earthlings*, and "Dancing Out in Space" plays on even rhythms, reeling off a new catchy refrain. The homage to the most experimental *Scott Walker* of the final *Heat* closes the circle, almost an appetizer of the sinister litanies of Blackstar. Completing the redemption of *The Next Day* are two brilliant videos directed by Floria Sigismondi: the irreverent (and censored) one for the title track, with Bowie in the role of a holy man singing in the nightclub *The Decameron*, flanked by an ineffable Gary Oldman-bishop and a disturbing Marion Cotillard, and that of *The Stars (Are Out Tonight)*, in which actress Tilda Swinton, with her ambiguous and androgynous charm, forms with David a surreal middle-class couple on the verge of a nervous breakdown, dealing with sensual and mysterious neighbors (the model Andrej Pejic and the pin-up Saskia de Brauw).

However, there will be no concert or promotional activity to support *The Next Day*. In a pseudo-interview, Bowie will limit himself to listing 42 words that in his opinion describe the album. But the emotion for his return will be so strong that it will project him to the top of the UK Chart (after 20 years!) and to no. 2 in the USA.

Meanwhile, London celebrates him with *David Bowie is*, the largest retrospective exhibition ever dedicated to his career, set up at the Victoria & Albert Museum and containing 300 objects from his private archive in New York: the sum of the 50-year career of a rock legend, through private letters, drawings, artwork, shots, and exclusive photos by Herb Ritts and Helmut Newton, in addition, of course, to his eccentric outfits.

2015

But time "waits in the wings and bends like a whore" (*Time*). And not even the one who has spent a lifetime playing against it can do anything to stop it. The hands of the clock run inexorably for David Bowie, who in mid-2014 was diagnosed with liver cancer. He spoke about it only to his family and a very few collaborators. A year later, in November 2015, the disease entered the terminal stage.

But if his life was a work of art, his death could not be any less. So, Bowie did not stop until the end. First, he managed to fulfill his dream of making a musical, which he had been cultivating since the days of Ziggy Stardust. The show *Lazarus*, cowritten with Irish screenwriter Enda Walsh, is a sort of sequel to *The Man Who Fell to Earth*, with Michael C. Hall (*Six Feet Under, Dexter*) in the lead role and many of the Thin White Duke's most beloved songs. During rehearsals, Bowie is often present, despite his grave health conditions. At the premiere in New York, on December 7, 2015, he goes onstage with the cast and the director to receive his last, triumphant standing ovation.

Michael C. Hall as Thomas Jerome Newton and Sophie Anne Caruso as Girl in the musical Lazarus *by David Bowie and Enda Walsh, directed by Ivo van Hove, at the Kings Cross Theatre in London, November 3, 2016*

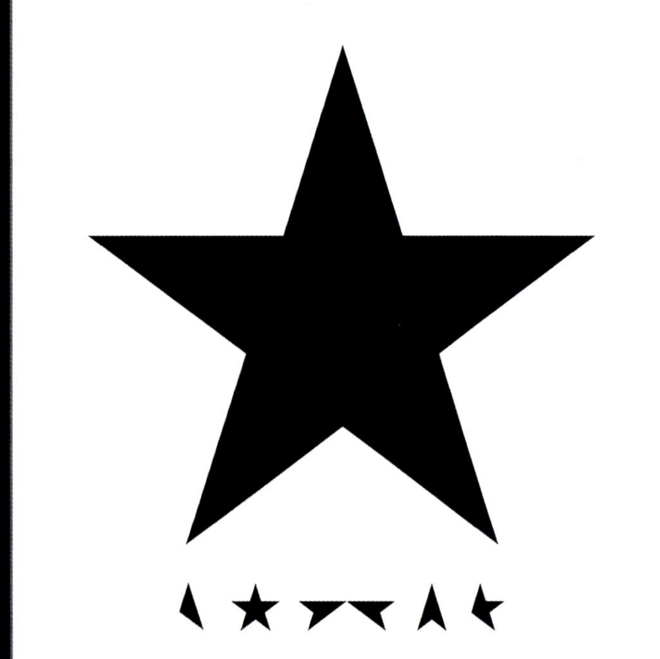

But that's not all, because "Lazarus" is also one of the songs that he will include in his testamentary album, recorded in great secrecy in New York, with Visconti and the jazz group of the saxophonist Donny McCaslin that he had discovered in a New York club (Jason Linder on keyboards, Mark Guiliana on drums, and Tim Lefebvre on bass). To say goodbye to the world, the Starman plans one last journey, on the sidereal routes that lead to his *Blackstar*, where he will return to being stardust. An album that for the first time does not reproduce his face on the cover, but only an emblematic black star on a white background, designed by Jonathan Barnbrook, offering a mysterious packaging, full of clues to be discovered.

Above: The cover of Blackstar, *David Bowie's parting-gift album, released on January 8, 2016, two days before his death*

The funereal title track was released first, destined to serve as the theme song for the TV series *The Last Panthers* by Johan Renck, who also created the enigmatic video in which Bowie plays a tormented blind character with buttons for eyes, a cheater and a disturbing preacher holding the book with the black star, while the skeleton of an astronaut floats in space until it falls into a black hole. Musically, it is a mutant jazz-soul-dance-ambient suite of almost ten minutes (the second-longest song of his career, after "Station to Station"), with arpeggios in the style of Radiohead-era *Kid A — Amnesiac*, drum machines in counter-tempo, sax solo, glam strings, and a hieratic crooning in the style of Walker, which seems to come from another galaxy. "Look up here, I'm in heaven / I've got scars that can't be seen," Bowie sings in the following single, "Lazarus": Propelled by an imperious bass à la Joy Division and by that nocturnal sax that acts as the glue for the entire album, the self-epitaph is accompanied by another lugubrious clip (again by Renck) in which Bowie appears emaciated and bandaged with rags, before disappearing into a closet. The end exorcised in an artistic key, knowing that he is already beyond, as he also announces in the melancholic ballad "Dollar Days," clinging to McCaslin's sax lines.

Despite the clues scattered throughout the album, the alarm bells don't go off in the listeners' ears, perhaps because a hint of death has always hovered in Bowie's lyrics ("The Width of a Circle," "Quicksand," "Five Year," the cover of Jacques Brel's "My Death," the B side of *Diamond Dogs, Dead Man Walking, Heathen,* "Where Are We Now?"). But this time it's not the paranoia of an alien trapped in a rock star's body or a new coup de théâtre to manipulate the world; it's the lucid awareness of a man who looks death in the face and doesn't back down.

Yet, Bowie does not lose his energy in episodes that bear his unmistakable mark, such as the tense liturgy of "Girl Loves Me," where Lefebvre's ostinato bass supports lines borrowed from the language invented by Anthony Burgess in *A Clockwork Orange*, the adrenaline-filled jazz-rock of "'Tis a Pity She Was a Whore" (from the title of an eighteenth-century tragedy by John Ford), with Guiliana's syncopated beat and tenor sax fueling a crescendo of acid grooves, and the pressing free jazz of "Sue (or in a Season of Crime)," which reinterprets the song in a darker, more electronic key in collaboration with American composer Maria Schneider, published in the collection *Nothing Has Changed* (2014). Up to the moving epilogue of "I Can't Give Everything Away," a blue-note pop suspended somewhere between "Life on Mars?" (the descending round of jazzy chords) and the Berlin fogs (the harmonica that recalls "A New Career in a New Town"), with a sumptuous arrangement for piano, sax, and strings pierced by Monder's only guitar solo on the album and with Bowie's peaceful singing, who takes his leave: "Saying no but meaning yes / This is all I ever meant / That's the message that I sent."

This is the real shock: All clichés are true; years really pass by; life is as short as they tell you

| DAVID BOWIE

Just when the world was cheering for his latest feat, the terrible news arrived: David Bowie passed away on January 10, 2016, after eighteen months of fighting cancer. "He always did what he wanted. And he always wanted to do it his way and in the best way," Visconti recalls. "His death was no different from his life, a work of art. He made *Blackstar* for us, as a gift. I had known for a year that it would go like this, but I wasn't prepared. He was an extraordinary man, full of love and life. He will always be with us. Now, however, it is right to mourn." On January 12, 2016, in accordance with his wishes, Bowie was cremated in New Jersey and his ashes were scattered according to Buddhist rituals in Bali, Indonesia. Among his testamentary provisions, there was also a bequest of two million dollars to Coco Schwab, his lifelong assistant.

At the news, *Blackstar* tops the charts in thirty-five countries (including the UK, Italy, and, for the first time, the US). All his records are plundered; his videos receive millions of views. And a wave of Bowiemania invades the planet. Homages, murals (the one with *Aladdin Sane* in Brixton is moving), and flash mobs multiply. The entire musical world celebrates him: Mick Jagger, Paul McCartney, Madonna, Kate Bush, the Who, Bruce Springsteen. An all-star cast takes part in the two tribute concerts at Carnegie Hall and Radio City Music Hall in New York (March 31 and April 1). Even NASA tweets, "The stars look very different today," quoting his "Space Oddity." To the list of "his" cities (London, New York, Berlin) that organize exhibitions and initiatives in his honor, we can add Paris, which even dedicated a street to him—Rue David Bowie, in the 13th arrondissement—on the occasion of what would have been his seventy-seventh birthday, on January 8, 2024.

And while Brett Morgen's documentary *Moonage Daydream* (2022)—the only one officially approved by his heirs—attempts to reconstruct his enigma through an immersive experience that is a sort of stream of consciousness in his mind, the inevitable series of posthumous albums also begins: the EP *No Plan* (2017), with "Lazarus" and three outtakes from the Blackstar sessions included in the soundtrack of the musical; the beloved *Toy*; multiple collections and box sets, including *Rock 'n' Roll Star* (2024), a box set packed with demos, alternative takes, and unreleased tracks from the Ziggy Stardust era.

Nothing, however, that can alleviate the sense of emptiness left by his disappearance. But if it is true, as Fred Frith and Howard Howe write in the essay "Art into Pop," that "Bowie is a black canvas on which people write their dreams," all that will remain will be to close our eyes to continue living suspended forever in his stardust.

Right and next pages: Flowers, messages, and mementos left by his fans next to his mural in Brixton, London

Jackie
Because m
Love for Y
Would break
heart i two
THANKYOU
Bowie

AUTHOR

CLAUDIO FABRETTI, journalist and music critic, graduated in Law at Sapienza University in Rome and specialized in Journalism at Luiss University in Rome. After working as an editor at the weekly magazine *Avvenimenti*, he has been at the free press *Leggo* since 2001, where he currently holds the role of editor-in-chief of the paper edition. He has collaborated with *Corriere dello Sport*, *Adnkronos*, *Kataweb*, *L'Espresso*, *Rockstar*, *Blow-Up*, and *Prog Italia*. Since 2001, he has directed the music webzine *OndaRock* and its cinematic twin *OndaCinema*. He hosts the music program *Rock in Onda* on the Roman station Radio Città Aperta. In 2011, he published his first book, *Francesco De Gregori. Between the Light Pages and the Dark Pages*, followed in 2012 by a volume on R.E.M., *Perfect Circle*, both for Arcana.

Special thanks to Marco Bercella, *OndaRock* collaborator and great Bowian expert, for his precious advice.

Photographic credits

Page 3: PA Images/Alamy Foto Stock
Page 5: Greg Gorman/Getty Images
Page 7: © Sukita
Page 9: © Sukita
Page 10: United Archives GmbH/Alamy Stock Photo
Pages 12-13: ©Sukita ©1977/1997 Risky Folio, Inc. Courtesy of The David Bowie Archive™
Page 15: Dave Hogan/Getty Images
Pages 20-21: Archivio GBB/Alamy Stock Photo
Page 22: Archivio GBB/Alamy Stock Photo
Page 24: Pictorial Press Ltd/Alamy Stock Photo
Page 25: Private Collection
Pages 26-27: Trinity Mirror/Mirrorpix/Alamy Stock Photo
Page 27: Pictorial Press Ltd/Alamy Stock Photo
Page 28: Private Collection
Page 29: Pictorial Press Ltd/Alamy Stock Photo
Page 31: Michael Ochs Archives/Getty Images
Page 33: Nobby Clark/Popperfoto/Getty Images
Page 34: Michael Ochs Archives/Getty Images
Page 35: Vinyls/Alamy Stock Photo
Page 36: Pictorial Press Ltd/Alamy Stock Photo
Page 37: Trinity Mirror/Mirrorpix/Alamy Stock Photo
Page 38: Rolf Adlercreutz/Alamy Stock Photo
Page 40: Private Collection
Page 41: Vinyls/Alamy Stock Photo
Page 42: David Lichtneker/Alamy Stock Photo
Page 43: Landmark Media/Alamy Stock Photo
Page 49: © Sukita
Page 51: Roger Bamber/Alamy Stock Photo
Page 53: © Sukita
Pages 54-55: Ilpo Musto/Alamy Stock Photo
Page 56: Watal Asanuma/Shinko Music/Getty Images
Pages 58-59: Ilpo Musto/Alamy Stock Photo
Page 61: Records/Alamy Stock Photo
Page 63: Records/Alamy Stock Photo
Page 64: Evening Standard/Hulton Archive/Getty Images
Page 66: Trinity Mirror/Mirrorpix/Alamy Stock Photo
Page 67: Steve Wood/Express/Getty Images
Page 69: David Lichtneker/Alamy Stock Photo

Page 70: RLFE Pix/Alamy Stock Photo
Page 73: Debi Doss/Hulton Archive/Getty Images
Page 75: Pictorial Press Ltd/Alamy Stock Photo
Pages 76-77: Gijsbert Hanekroot/Alamy Stock Photo
Pages 78-79: Gijsbert Hanekroot/Redferns/Getty Images
Page 80: Pictorial Press Ltd/Alamy Stock Photo
Page 81: Private Collection
Page 87: Ron Galella/WireImage/Getty Images
Page 89: David Lichtneker/Alamy Stock Photo
Pages 90-91: Michael Ochs Archives/Getty Images
Page 92: Private Collection
Page 94: Michael Putland/Getty Images
Page 96: Michael Putland/Getty Images
Page 97: Jorgen Angel/Redferns/Getty Images
Page 98: Jan Persson/Getty Images
Page 99: Evening Standard/Getty Images
Page 100: Christian Simonpietri/Sygma/Getty Images
Page 101: Chalkie Davies/Getty Images
Page 103: Steve Wood/Popperfoto/Getty Images
Page 106 left: David Lichtneker / Alamy Stock Photo
Page 106 right: Express Newspapers/Getty Images
Page 107: Christian Simonpietri/Sygma/Getty Images
Page 109: Records/Alamy Stock Photo
Page 112: Rajko Simunovic/Alamy Stock Photos
Page 115: Daily Mirror/Mirrorpix/Mirrorpix via Getty Images
Page 119: Photo Duffy © Duffy Archive
Page 121: Acorn 1/Alamy Stock Photo
Page 122: Private Collection
Page 123: Records/Alamy Stock Photo
Page 124: Albert Foster/Mirrorpix/Getty Images
Page 126: Records/Alamy Stock Photo
Page 127: Walter McBride/Corbis/Getty Images
Page 128: Records/Alamy Stock Photo
Page 129 left: David Lichtneker/Alamy Stock Photo
Page 129: Records/Alamy Stock Photo
Pages 130-131: Denis O'Regan/Getty Images
Page 132: Michael Putland/Getty Images
Page 133: Rob Verhorst/Redferns/Getty Images
Page 134: Private Collection
Page 136: Georges De Keerle/Getty Images
Page 137: Records/Alamy Stock Photo
Page 138: Gie Knaeps/Getty Images
Page 139: Denis O'Regan/Getty Images
Pages 140-141: Gie Knaeps/Getty Images
Page 142: Pictorial Press Ltd/Alamy Stock Photo
Page 147: dpa picture alliance/Alamy Stock Photo
Pages 148-149: Keystone Press/Alamy Stock Photo
Page 150: Vinyls/Alamy Stock Photo
Page 151: Lester Cohen/Getty Images
Page 153: Private Collection
Page 154: The Asahi Shimbun/Getty Images
Page 155: Private Collection
Page 156: Ron Galella/Getty Images
Page 157: Private Collection
Page 162: Private Collection
Page 163: Allstar Picture Library/Alamy Stock Photo
Page 167: KMazur/WireImage/Getty Images
Page 169: Nicky J. Sims/Redferns Getty Images
Page 172: Screen Archives/Getty Images
Page 174: Moviestore Collection Ltd/Alamy Stock Photo
Page 175: Photo 12/Alamy Stock Photo
Page 176: ScreenProd/Photononstop/Alamy Stock Photo
Page 177: United Archives GmbH/Alamy Stock Photo
Pages 178-179: Allstar Picture Library Limited/Alamy Stock Photo
Page 180: United Archives GmbH/Alamy Stock Photo
Page 181: Miramax Films/Everett Collection/Bridgeman Images
Page 182: ScreenProd/Photononstop/Alamy Stock Photo
Page 183: Maximum Film/Alamy Stock Photo
Page 187: Hayley Madden/Redferns/Getty Images
Page 188: Private Collection
Pages 190-191: KMazur/WireImag/Getty Images
Pages 192-193: KMazur/WireImag/Getty Images
Page 195: Private Collection
Pages 196-197: KMazur/WireImag/Getty Images
Page 198: Private Collection
Pages 200-201: Robbie Jack/Corbis/Getty Images
Page 202: Private Collection
Page 205: chrisdorney/Shutterstock
Page 206-207: PA Images/Alamy Stock Photo

Unofficial and unauthorized

Piazzale Luigi Cadorna, 6
20123 Milan, Italy
www.whitestar.it.

Library of Congress Control Number: 2025939981

Designed by Paola Piacco
Cover design by Molly Shields
Project editor: Valeria Manferto / Consulting D&D
Translated from the Italian by Inga Sempel
Editor: Phillip Gaskill

ISBN: 978-0-7643-7103-5

Printed in China
10 9 8 7 6 5 4 3 2 1

Published by Schiffer Publishing, Ltd.
4880 Lower Valley Road
Atglen, PA 19310
Phone: (610) 593-1777; Fax: (610) 593-2002
Email: info@schifferbooks.com
Web: www.schifferbooks.com